HOW TO SELL Y
AND LIVE HAPPILY EVER AFTER

For a complete list of Management Books 2000 titles,
visit our web-site at http://www.mb2000.com

HOW TO SELL YOUR BUSINESS AND LIVE HAPPILY EVER AFTER

Gary Morley

2000

First edition published 1997
This new edition published 1999 by Management Books 2000 Ltd
Cowcombe House,
Cowcombe Hill,
Chalford,
Gloucestershire GL6 8HP
Tel. 01285-760722 Fax: 01285-760708
e-mail: MB2000@compuserve.com

Printed and bound in Great Britain by Biddles, Guildford

British Library Cataloguing in Publication Data is available

ISBN 1-85252-273-9

Preface

This book gives straightforward, practical advice on selling your business, including the tax implications, and is a comprehensive preparation for the complex issues involved. You will, of course, also need professional advice specific to your own case, but read what follows before you take any further steps, and use the book as an aide-mémoire during the selling process. Tell your advisers you are reading it – it will keep them on their toes!

Acknowledgements

I'd very much like to thank Guy Rigby for doing the proof reading and for his (unsolicited) comments, Nigel Landsman for helping update the tax chapter, Zoe Ryder for managing me and the project (all of MacIntyre Corporate Finance), and Michael Edwards of Edwin Coe for providing the Sale and Purchase Agreement set out in Appendix .V

Contents

Introduction

Selling your business is probably the biggest financial undertaking of your life. You have only one chance to get it right. Getting it even slightly wrong can substantially affect your future.

As a business person, you may be faced with dozens of decisions every day, yet it is likely that all the decisions you make in the course of a year combined are less important than the right decision on selling your company.

First, what do you want to achieve? If your answer is, simply, "the biggest possible cheque", that's fine. But how would you feel if the existing operations were shut down, the name changed and the business transferred to some far-off enterprise zone? Would you have preferred the business to prosper relatively unchanged? Is it important to protect some or all of the employees? Do you want to remain involved on a part-time basis?

Knowing when to sell is also important. Few businesses show good profits over long periods. The perfect time to sell is usually when the profit cycle approaches its peak. It is therefore best to plan your intended sale well ahead.

How will you know if you have got the best possible price? There are many examples of companies being purchased and then sold soon afterwards at a huge profit. Also, if the highest price means having to wait for some of the money, the financial standing of the purchaser has to be considered – even highly respected public companies can suddenly go bust.

So you need to ensure that you achieve the best deal. You have no experience in valuing a business or negotiating a transaction with so many variables and which can be structured in so many different ways. The tax implications and the requirements of the Companies Acts are a labyrinth. And while all this is going on you have a business to run. How do you do it?

1

Appointing an Adviser

*Never believe what you hear,
and only half believe what you see*

The first step is to appoint an advisor who will help with the
technical side of things and steer you through the process with
a mindful eye to the many potential pitfalls along the way.
There are many professionals who claim to offer expertise in
this area, ranging from county solicitors through to fully-
fledged City merchant banks, and not all of them can always
deliver the service you might expect.

One common method of trying to sell a business is by
approaching the company's auditors or (even worse) the
family solicitor. Most professional firms with under a hundred
staff do not have Corporate Finance specialists. This, however,
will not stop them from eagerly undertaking the assignment, as
they believe it is relatively easy and it is their last chance to earn
significant fees from a departing client!

Without a Corporate Finance specialist, the partner or
manager undertaking the work will not have the experience

either to market the business or to negotiate the best terms on your behalf. They will do some research into the obvious buyers of the business, and if that comes to nought (as it usually does), they flounder: they are trying to learn how to sell a business on the back of your fees. One of the biggest obstacles for Corporate Finance specialists in getting appointed is the complaint from the vendor that he has already spent considerable amounts of money by using his own accountant or solicitor, and has got nowhere. A poor intermediary can do harm: if there are time pressures on the vendor, some of that time has now been wasted; also, suitable purchasers have possibly been put off by badly handled approaches, and to approach them again would make you appear desperate.

Unless you enjoy paying large professional fees, never appoint anyone to act on the sale of your business who charges on a time basis. It is only in their interest to procrastinate, create unnecessary meetings and attend necessary meetings unnecessarily. "It's all good chargeable time" is a well-known professional phrase.

So how do you select an adviser?...

Track record: in a nutshell, this is what really matters. In the UK anyone can put a brass plate outside their door and advise on Mergers and Acquisitions – and it appears anyone does. If your intermediary does not have the right contacts and experience in doing deals, you will be wasting your time unless you (and he) are very lucky.

A good intermediary will have connections both in this country and overseas (especially in the EU and USA) with Merchant Banks, Corporate Finance specialists of the larger accountancy firms and other professional intermediaries. A good intermediary will know how to produce a good Information Memorandum; how to market a company confidentially; how to approach a prospective purchaser and reach the appropriate decision maker; how to present your

12

business; how to identify time-wasters; and how to construct and deliver a short-list of interested, suitable and financially capable potential purchasers.

A good intermediary will have the ability and experience to overcome obstacles to the purchaser, either real or imagined, generated by the purchaser's solicitor. The purchaser's solicitor himself can usually also overcome these – if you are prepared to accept a lower price for your business!

Every intermediary will tell you, and probably very articulately, that he can do all the above and more. It is a case not of buyer beware, but of seller beware.

It is essential to meet with several intermediaries at their premises. This will allow you to judge their professionalism and choose the one you feel confident and comfortable with. You must meet and have your discussions with the person who would actually be doing the work. It is no good meeting the top man who may be authoritative and impressive in his presentation to you and who may be entitled "lead partner" or "controlling partner" but whom you would never see again. After the groundwork of finding potential buyers, the relationship between you and the intermediary can become very intense as important meetings become scheduled, and de-briefing sessions at your home or on the telephone late into the evening become common. The intermediary becomes aware of very personal details about you and your lifestyle – your wife's hobbies, what time you go to bed, what book your grand-daughter is reading. This level of closeness is inevitable, and therefore you must have confidence in your adviser. You don't have to like him, but you do have to trust him and be able to work with him.

When you meet the intermediary, you should obviously question him on his experience, on the experience of the Corporate Finance department and on his view of the prospects and methodology of getting a good price for your business; you should also get to know him as a person, because you are going to be working very closely with him. Questions should be searching. How many deals does he do each year? How many deals is he currently working on? How often has he been unable to find a suitable buyer? How long has he been in business? How did he become involved in corporate finance?

The intermediary with first-hand experience in the real world of making acquisitions and disposals will have a distinct advantage. He will better understand the motivations, fears and practical considerations of the purchaser. Being forearmed, he will be in a better position to take advantage of opportunities and overcome obstacles. Many professional advisers have for all their working lives only been advisers. They have no idea what it is like actually making the decision to spend a significant amount of their own or their company's money. It can be a very chastening experience. The adage "those who can, do; those who can't, teach" is very appropriate in the corporate finance profession.

Some intermediaries claim to be industry specialists, and you may feel more comfortable with someone who can speak your language and knows the jargon. The problem with industry specialists is that usually they know only the obvious buyers – whom you probably already know yourself – so if all they can do is approach those people to buy your business (with the attached inherent risks – see "Obvious purchasers", page 26), they are not contributing very much to the transaction. What you need is someone whose speciality is selling businesses, regardless of the particular sector concerned.

A very important consideration is that the intermediary is professionally qualified as an accountant or solicitor and that he is part of a substantial firm. This should ensure a minimum professional standard and to some extent be self-policing, since an established firm would not risk its reputation by having an incompetent adviser working on your behalf. It also allows for a firm of substance to be sued if things go wrong – particularly for poor tax advice.

A firm active in Corporate Finance will probably be a

member of the British Venture Capital Association as a large part of most Corporate Finance activity is connected in some way with raising finance.

Think very carefully, also, about the solicitor you are going to use. Many people, even experienced business people, think every solicitor has a thorough understanding of every aspect of the law. It just ain't so! Solicitors specialise, like other professionals. If you were going blind you would be referred to an eye specialist. Your friend, the eminent heart surgeon, wouldn't come into it, but neither would he want to – and that is the difference! There are many specialist solicitors: those in banking law, in international shipping law, in franchise law, and of course in corporate law, but the danger is that if you go to own your solicitor – the family friend who did your house conveyancing and prepared your will – he will express himself as only too glad to act for you in a matter on which he has absolutely no experience. This can cost dearly. Inexperienced solicitors do not always protect their clients' best interests because not only might they miss an important point (and the purchaser's experienced corporate lawyer can quickly smell inexperience on the other side and milk it for all it's worth), but they might also argue *ad nauseam* over some incidental point that any reasonable corporate solicitor would accept without question, with obvious implications for your ultimate costs. In such circumstances it is not uncommon for your legal fees to be greater than those of the purchaser – and it is his solicitor who has to draw up the contract and undertake all the legal due diligence. It has also been known for the purchasers to withdraw out of frustration at not being able to come to a reasonable Sale and Purchase Agreement with an obstinate (for invalid reasons) solicitor. If you want to be properly protected, remember the advantages of using an experienced corporate lawyer.

Fees

Everything is negotiable. Haggle if you want to, although it will be far cheaper in the long run to get the right intermediary at seemingly higher fees than a bad intermediary at lower ones. Don't be tempted to use an intermediary who will act for you for nothing, stating that he will get the fee from the purchaser. The maxim "There's no such thing as a free lunch" is oh, so true of advisers! Obviously the purchaser will not pay any more, overall, than he thinks the business is worth to him, so if he has to pay the intermediary he will pay you less. But, more importantly, if the intermediary has a financial arrangement with the purchaser he will be acting in his interest rather than in yours. Worse still, from his perspective the selling of your business becomes a numbers game – he will want to place your details in front of as many people as possible, with the result that you will waste a considerable amount of time and energy seeing unsuitable purchasers. Such intermediaries need have little regard to the quality of their advice when this happens; and that means you are the loser.

The intermediary's fees should be substantially success-orientated. If they aren't, forget it. If the intermediary does not have faith in his ability to deliver, how can you?

By and large, fees in the industry work to the "Lehman Scale" – 5% of the first million pounds paid, 4% of the next, 3% of the third, 2% of the fourth, and 1% of anything above. In addition, there is usually a relatively small monthly retainer paid to the intermediary. This will not represent anything close to the time costs of the intermediary, but is in reality a commitment fee. The owner of a business might appoint an intermediary on a success-only basis, then, when it comes to the crunch with an offer on the table, change his mind and turn it down. This would be unfair on the intermediary, who would have done a lot of work for nothing. Also, if another client who was paying a retainer had demands which conflicted with yours, there would be a moral and practical obligation to put the paying client first, and with several paying clients, your requirements would have a low priority. Not only can the refusal to pay a retainer be a false economy, but you should be very dubious about appointing any intermediary who will work without such a commitment fee – he is obviously all too desperate for your business.

Advice on the taxation aspects of the sale are sometimes included in the success fee and should come only from a professionally qualified person – and you should always get it in writing.

One last thought – if you think professional fees can cost a lot, try out the amateur variety!

2

Preparing for Sale

Life is what happens to you while you are making plans for it

Think long and hard about what you want to achieve from selling your business. It is worth spending time on this. You may want to discuss it over several months with your spouse, fellow directors and minority shareholders.

You are facing the biggest financial decision of your life. You need to plan it. You need to know what you will do with the money. You need to know what you will do afterwards; even perhaps what your spouse is going to do. Only then can you be properly advised on how to achieve it. Once you have established your criteria, you can then start doing what is necessary.

With only a little foresight you can change some of the things that you do or don't do within your business, and thereby enhance its value. Longer-term planning can enhance its value still further. A number of possible courses of action are set out below. Of course, you don't have to do any of the things suggested – it's your business, and your money!

The quickest way to improve profitability is to stop any

"private" expenditure. This could be your private plane, your mother-in-law's Mercedes (or Mini), the gardener, "business" trips or the dining out. It is possible to explain all these things to a prospective purchaser, but then they will have to be itemised and agreed upon. It also means "washing your dirty linen in public". The sooner you stop the perks the better. There have been cases where the former owners of a business were sued to pay back expenditure of this kind as they are not true business expenses.

You should pay yourself as if you were an employee, at a rate commensurate with your position. This does not mean you have to lower your standard of living – you can simply switch to paying monthly dividends. The tax differential between salary and dividends is now fairly minimal, but this will boost the reported profits of your company. The viability of paying dividends will depend on who owns the shares. If you (and your spouse) don't own them all you will need the minority shareholders to agree to waive their rights to these extra dividends which are being paid to increase the value of their shares.

If your company qualifies you should consider re-registering your company as a PLC (it basically means a minimum of £50,000 distributable reserves and share capital). This gives an impression of success and stability. Even if you decide not to sell, the effect on customers, suppliers, competitors and staff will still be of benefit. The requirements are not onerous, and the direct costs of registering should be below £500. You will also have the additional costs of reprinting stationery and promotional material.

You should use the audited accounts as a showcase for your business. Don't take advantage of any of the reduced reporting requirements. Include a Chairman's Statement – expand the definition of Principal Activity in the Directors' Report – boast about what you have achieved and where the company is going. Freehold property (and other significant fixed assets) should be revalued, if appropriate, to reflect their enhanced value. Sell any redundant assets. If you are planning far enough ahead, write off any goodwill in your balance sheet so that it does not affect profits at the time of the sale.

The accounting policies should be reviewed to report maximum profits. This is often the opposite of what a family company tries to achieve to mitigate tax.

The controls and measurement of company performance should become formalised. You should implement budgetary controls and management accounts and ideally have several years' practice at this before selling, so that you know where your business is and the direction it is taking. This is particularly important if you sell your business on an "earn-out", where a proportion of the consideration is paid later on the basis of future profits. It will also help to demonstrate the underlying potential of the business to a prospective purchaser.

You should also at an early stage remove any dead wood including poorly performing staff. Apart from the obvious benefit to the company, a new owner will do it anyway, and it may affect earn-out calculations. You may feel it is better for all concerned for you to come to an arrangement now with staff who the company has outgrown rather than leaving them to be dismissed by the new owner with minimum compensation.

Give staff proper titles for the jobs they are doing. Have meetings and decisions minuted. This shows that there is management, structure and control in the business.

As with most things in life, presentation can be more important than content. How your company is presented can have an inordinate effect on how much purchasers will pay for it.

Finally, make sure that the shareholding structure of the company is as simple as possible. Minority interests, in particular, should be taken out wherever possible. By and large, purchasers do not like the inconvenience of having minority shareholders, and will therefore want to acquire one hundred per cent of the company. There can be difficulties in having to deal with several vendors and the need to come to decisions acceptable to all. The other shareholders may have a different set of objectives from yours. The minority shareholders, if they are employed in the business, may want an "executive style" ongoing employment contract which would be expensive for the new owners to break – this reduces the value of the business to the purchasers, and the burden falls disproportionately on you. It may be that the minority shareholders are not dependent on the sale proceeds. In such circumstances it has been known for them to demand a higher price for their shares, as they know you need to sell, and if this is not forthcoming they might veto a sale. The purchaser isn't going to pay more for the company and, in such circumstances, you are the one who will have to cough up.

If potential conflict with minority shareholders does exist, then before negotiations begin with any prospective purchaser you would be strongly advised to obtain a legally binding option from them for a period of, say, eighteen months, to allow you to purchase their shares and re-sell them on the same terms as you are selling your own. This is a no-gain-no-loss arrangement, but it allows you to deliver one hundred per cent of the share capital to a purchaser.

The Companies Acts do allow minority shareholdings of under ten per cent in total to be compulsorily purchased in a takeover, but the legal costs make this prohibitively expensive other than in large deals, and the purchaser would expect you to foot the bill.

If differing objectives do exist between the shareholders, a compromise could be achieved. For example, the deal could be structured so that the director/shareholders participate in an earn-out while the passive shareholders take a higher proportion of the initial consideration. Where there is goodwill between the shareholders, an experienced intermediary should be able to produce a satisfactory settlement for all concerned.

3

Finding a Purchaser

God save me from my friends;
from my enemies I can save myself.

There are several ways of going about finding a purchaser:

- Advertising
- Approaching competitors
- Approaching suppliers or distributors who may be interested in "vertical integration"
- Approaching individual or corporate investors who might have an interest in adding your company to their portfolio
- Looking for overseas purchasers interested in territorial expansion

Advertising

You might think, once you have decided to sell your business, that a cheap and easy way to start would be to place a simple newspaper advertisement. This probably spells disaster!

This is how things can go wrong if you advertise. You are inundated with enquiries: they come from competitors (usually in disguise); people with no money; corporate vultures; time-wasters; second-rate intermediaries who suspect you need help and want to capitalise on your naivety; and, just possibly, genuine potential purchasers. You don't know what to do. You try to pick out the best respondents, you meet several and waste a lot of time. This takes you away from managing your business, which costs you money. Your staff become concerned at the parade of visitors to your premises. Your chief accountant twigs that something is afoot when he receives repeated requests for information from different visitors, which leads him to conclude that you must be selling the business. The cat is out of the bag. Once one person within a company knows, everyone knows.

Staff do not like the uncertainty of change. They don't know who they will be working for, or whether they may be made redundant. Your best people (and especially your good salespeople) may start applying for jobs with your competitors, who quickly learn their reasons for wanting to leave. Your competitors tell their salesmen, who in turn tell your customers, that you are having to sell out because: (a) you are going bust and/or the bank is no longer willing to support you, and therefore you cannot be relied upon for deliveries; (b) you have to sell to settle gambling debts or to meet calls from the several Lloyds syndicates to which you belong; (c) you are going to emigrate to San Francisco with a young boy from the tennis club; or (d) you've got a social disease...

However it is put, it will give your competitors an edge, as by this time they have taken on your sales staff, and your customers will want a reliable supplier.

The loss of staff, and the low morale of those who remain, will affect your business. This, together with the amount of your time taken up meeting the respondents to the advertisement can have a dire effect – within a short time your monthly management accounts show worsening results and any genuine prospective purchaser thinks you are selling out just before the bubble bursts. Not the best climate in which to secure a good deal.

Almost as a knee-jerk reaction, many people do place an advertisement in *The Financial Times* to try to sell their business. This is an excellent newspaper, but it is not the place to sell a business. Most of the companies advertised for sale there are in receivership. In these cases it does not matter what the staff or competitors think: it's too late for that. It is doubtful whether many businesses advertised in *The Financial Times* – other than those in receivership – end up with the best deal for the vendor.

Flotation

Some sellers of business are led into believing that the best way to achieve a successful sale is by floating it on the Stock Exchange or junior markets such as AIM (Alternative Investment Market) or Ofex. This is anything but a sale. If what you want to achieve is simply a small percentage of the value of your business in hard cash and to continue working hard then flotation may, and only may, be appropriate. The downsides to such a route are:

(a) Your fortunes and that of your business are subject to the vagaries of stock market sentiment as a whole and therefore out of your control: for example, Monsoon plc floated (on the main London Stock Exchange) in February 1998 at a price of 195p per share – announced their financial results in September 1998 which were exactly as they had forecast when they floated – and the shares were valued 65% lower at 67p.

(b) After the flotation it will be difficult for you to raise any further significant money from the sale of your shares without disastrously affecting the share price (unless you sell all of your remaining holding).

(c) It is never certain that the vast amount of legal, financial and management work involved in grooming the company will actually result in a flotation. This can waste a substantial amount of your time and money, as well as demoralising for your staff and potentially damaging the value of the company should you then want to sell it.

(d) You and your top management will have to spend time on "City" matters that have nothing to do with your business. You will also have to brief stock market analysts and explain your results and decisions in far more detail than you have done to anyone in the past. Your company will be constantly scrutinised so that any mistake will be made public for all to see. Even removing a director of the company will have to be considered in the context of how it will be interpreted by the "City".

(e) The business will have to incur significant additional costs each year producing glossy financial statements, employing more expensive auditors, financial PR consultants etc.

(f) You must continue to show significant profit growth year after year or become "dead stock".

Flotation is an ideal route in specific circumstances but definitely not if your objectives are to secure your financial future or for you and your family to enjoy the spoils of your success.

Obvious purchasers

An "obvious" purchaser for your business is one who operates in the same or a similar business, whether vertically or horizontally. You know of him, and he probably knows of you. An obvious purchaser is usually either a competitor or a potential competitor.

Such potential purchasers could be good news. They will already understand your business, causing less disruption in getting to know it and making lower demands on your time. The potential for cost savings which could be made on a takeover will be more apparent (and probably more obtainable) to them, and therefore they may be able to pay a higher price. They will probably be able to eliminate some overheads, such as the accounts department, or even the General Manager. Depending on the rationale for their interest, they may be able to eliminate selling costs by using their own sales force to sell your product along with their own. They may want to utilise your spare capacity by shifting their production to your premises, thereby saving on the rent and rates of premises that they vacate. There may be economies of scale in production or in bulk buying power. Clearly, most businesses will have very great attractions to an obvious purchaser.

However, obvious purchasers may not be willing to pay you a premium for the savings that they are going to make. The reverse is often true: most obvious purchasers will know your weaknesses and play on them – this is particularly true if they are aware of pressures on you to sell. Direct competitors will probably already know who your major customers are, who your suppliers are and how your company operates. Why should they pay a premium for it? They may believe, particularly in a business that operates in a niche market, that they are the only potential purchasers because they have checked out any other obvious purchasers. In such circumstances it is unlikely that they are going to make a generous offer. It is therefore dangerous to your wealth to limit the marketing of your business solely to obvious purchasers.

Because obvious purchasers will usually be competitors, the releasing of commercial information to them must be of serious concern. Even the very fact that the company is for sale can cause it irreparable damage. Notwithstanding that the competitor has signed a confidentiality undertaking this can not in practice stop a whispering campaign, and the onus of proof of any breach of confidentiality would be on you.

A further major disadvantage of directing the sale of your business only to obvious purchasers is that it unnecessarily limits your options. There are many potential purchasers whom you could not possibly know, each with their own criteria or acquisition – and your company may fit these criteria. Confidential professional marketing of your business by a good intermediary should provide you with a short-list of active acquirers who want to buy your business.

A couple of examples will probably best illustrate the point:

i)   A computer software company purchased a double-glazing window manufacturer. The reason: The computer software company had sold its business and assets (as opposed to selling the shares). This meant that for tax purposes it was advantageous for it to buy a business that had freehold premises and substantial plant and equipment (so it could roll-over the gain and defer paying tax). The owner of the company was really a sales-orientated person who had "fallen into" the software business. He saw the potential that the double-glazing window manufacturer would have with a stronger sales and marketing approach. He could provide that strength and the tax would also be saved, so his company bought the business.

ii) A council services contractor sold its business to a medium-sized quoted healthcare company. The contractor knew all the obvious purchasers, but for reasons of confidentiality appointed an intermediary to front the situation, supplying him with a list of their names. The contractor ideally wanted £4m. None of the obvious purchasers were interested as it was too expensive. The intermediary introduced the quoted healthcare company, who paid £9m. The reason: the quoted company needed both to diversify and to improve the quality of its earnings; the contractor had good profitable contracts with councils for up to five years ahead, and the price paid was lower than its P/E ratio and therefore did not dilute its earnings per share.

There is of course nothing wrong in selling your business to an obvious purchaser, but the relative risks must be weighed against the possible rewards.

Management Buy-Outs

Another big danger is trying to sell your business to your own staff – commonly known as a Management Buy-Out ("MBO"). Whilst it is true that there are many successful high profile MBOs where the value of the deal is in excess of £50 million, what isn't widely known is the disastrous effects that can occur when owners of smaller companies begin to negotiate with their key staff who want to buy their businesses.

Immediately, the loyal and dedicated staff you have known for years suddenly have goals that are opposite to yours. They do not want to maximise the value of the business to you; they want to minimise it for them. It is in their interest to reduce profitability (in the short term) and thus reduce the price. You have created the "Enemy Within".

The danger of the Enemy Within cannot be overstated. Once the possibility of riches beyond their dreams takes hold, even your most decent and upright member of staff can, and often does, become unscrupulous. The whole management team can become unscrupulous. It is their big chance. The following is a true story:

A large diverse private group decided to have a more focussed direction. The management of one of the subsidiaries (which was in security and access control) saw what was happening and began, in a very ruthless way, to

29

turn the profits into losses. They even made the gross profit into a loss! They then made an offer to buy the company. The holding company knew something was amiss but not what. The holding company decided, as a point of principle that they would not sell the company to the management team; who then left. The company, void of any management, was sold to a competitor for £1. The new owner put his accounting systems in place and discovered undervalued stocks and work in progress and substantial under invoicing; he found in excess of £500,000 which he did not expect to receive!

Even if you have absolute faith in the integrity of your staff, that only overcomes one of the impediments to a successful MBO. You will have several parties with whom you have to negotiate.

First, there is the management team. This is not usually the easiest of discussions. You will clearly be extolling the virtues of the company and its very bright future, whilst your staff will be putting to you its shortcomings and other hard-hitting home truths. Can you imagine having such a meeting with your three most senior managers and how it would affect the ongoing management of the business?

Also, it is not uncommon for the MBO team to have disagreements between themselves and fall out; that also does not help with the ongoing management of the business. The MBO team will need to have a deal agreed, in broad terms, before they can start the arduous exercise of actually raising the money to fund the purchase.

Except for very small deals, the funding will invariably come from Venture Capitalists ("VCs"). VC funds now like to be known as Private Equity providers probably because it sounds softer and easier to deal with, and the word venture can easily be mistaken for the word vulture! They are, however, still as shrewd and as calculating as ever.

Once the VCs are involved they will virtually always want

to renegotiate the deal – and *not* (surprise, surprise) in your favour! At this stage it will be impossible to get alternative competitive bids from trade buyers as meetings with the MBO team will hardly be conducive to a positive view on the suitability and value of the proposed acquisition.

The MBO team may, at an early stage, produce a letter from a VC purporting to support the deal. Read the letter clearly and you will see it means nothing more than that the VC is happy to look at the proposal or any other proposal that may come along. Some VCs issue these letters to prospective MBO teams before the initial approach to the owners. It is not and cannot be regarded as any commitment at all.

VCs will not commit to funding a deal unless they are fully satisfied with a) the terms of the deal with you, b) the soundness of the business, c) the abilities of the management team and d) the terms of their deal with the management team.

On these points, VCs much prefer to back a team rather than an individual. They like to see that the team has the skills of leadership, finance, sales and operations. VCs also have a requirement that each member of the team puts some of his own money at risk in funding the deal. This "hurt" money is useful a) as an indication of commitment to the deal and b) to tie them into the deal so that they have the same objectives as the VCs and makes it difficult for them to leave the venture. The hurt money can usually only come from one source: remortgaging the family home. No matter how gung-ho the MBO team member might be in becoming his own boss, his spouse can take a very different view of risk when she has to sign away the family home.

Many MBO teams (as well as the vendors of the business) do not realise at the outset that a substantial part of any VC funds used for an MBO are lent to the business as secured loans which attract interest. The result is a highly geared business which means that for the next 3 to 7 years virtually all the profits generated by the business are used to fund the interest and capital repayments on the loans.

It is a fact that less than 10% of proposals put to VCs actually result in a deal. So, possibly through no fault of their own, the MBO team fail in their bid for your business – it will have taken up a considerable amount of time and money from your most key staff. How now will the business have been affected? How demotivated and demoralised will your key staff be? How now will an outside prospective purchaser view the value of your business?

You have been warned.

Less obvious purchasers

Finding less obvious purchasers is much more difficult, and this is where a good intermediary with expertise in mergers and acquisitions, and a network of active contacts, can be particularly useful. Often these kind of transactions develop on the basis of word-of-mouth – with contact made through informal or "networked" channels.

An experienced intermediary will have a host of different contacts and potential purchasers simply by being in the business of mergers and acquisitions. Acquisitive individuals and companies are in constant contact with merger and acquisition specialists to ensure that should a suitable target become available, then they will have an early opportunity to consider it.

The titanic expansion of the Alternative Investment Market ("AIM") and the smaller and less regulated Ofex market has created a plethora of companies that sorely need to use their (relatively) highly rated quoted shares to make acquisitions. It is the way of the stock markets that unless a company produces above average growth then the value of its shares drops like a stone into the abyss, often never to return. Acquisitions are a classic method of producing growth. So here is a potential fountain of possible purchasers but unless you are connected to them or their stockbrokers it is unlikely that you will know who might be suitable to acquire your business.

Research

If you are insistent on doing the spadework yourself there are several sources of information – sometimes overlapping, sometimes complimentary.

Most large libraries have directories of businesses, such as Kompass, which list businesses both by geographical location and by commercial activity. Such directories are better at some industry sectors than at others – check to see whether your business is listed.

If you think that your business may be suited to a quoted company, then McCarthys is useful for finding out the latest information. The larger public libraries often have the latest annual report and financial statements of quoted companies – useful to find out the name of the chairman or financial director to contact.

Don't forget Yellow Pages – also often found in the larger public libraries. Also trade journals/magazines for your industry often report on who's acquired who – but be careful not to limit your search to "obvious" sectors only (see above).

The national company search agents such as Infocheck and Dun & Bradstreet can do searches on information held at Companies House using criteria such as turnover, postcodes and the standard industry classification (SIC) code on the annual return.

The accountancy firm, KPMG, and the magazine Acquisitions Monthly produce lists of recent acquisitions and disposals showing, inter alia, the size of the deals and the parties concerned. This may be a good starting point but by the very nature of such lists not all transactions are reported.

If you are on the Internet – well, the world is your lobster. You can spend many afternoons and evenings surfing away amassing huge amounts of data. A good place to start is www.dis.strath.ac.uk/business/index.html run by The University of Strathclyde which gives a selective guide to Internet sites which contain business information.

However, never forget that no matter how thorough and

detailed your research is, you will only ever be identifying companies which *you* think may be interested in acquiring you. You will not produce a list of potential purchasers who *themselves* think they are interested in acquiring you. Companies who you think should be interested may not actually be interested at all, while there may well be potential purchasers out there who have their own reasons for being interested in acquiring you which you could not begin to anticipate!

Making the approach

In most instances an approach from a professional intermediary has a better chance of success than a cold approach from the vendor in person – for much the same reason that a publisher will be more receptive to a proposal from a literary agent than from an unpublished author. The fact that a professional intermediary has endorsed the proposal by taking it on in the first place adds weight to the proposal itself; the indirect approach also enables a potential investor (or publisher) to assess the proposal without fear of being dragged into a difficult personal correspondence if the proposal is rejected.

Obviously there are exceptions to this rule; where the target is already known personally to the vendor, it clearly makes sense to build on this existing relationship with a direct approach. However, it can still be advantageous to hand over the grittier aspects of negotiations to a third party.

Confidentiality undertaking

Whichever way you find a potential buyer it is essential that you get an appropriate confidentiality undertaking from them before divulging any information. An intermediary would be able to get a confidentiality undertaking prior to them even knowing the name of your company. Do not think that such an undertaking will protect your business from unscrupulous operators (so always be cautious in revealing information) but it is far better to have one than not.

Appendix IV gives an example of a confidentiality undertaking.

4

The Information Memorandum

Even hot cakes have to be sold

The Information Memorandum, sometimes called a prospectus, is normally prepared by the intermediary as part of his overall service, and included in his fee.

The Information Memorandum is primarily a selling document. It should present your business in the most favourable way, highlighting its strengths and minimising its weaknesses. It should also be comprehensive enough to answer all the questions a prospective purchaser needs to ask. This will save you time, as you will then meet only those who have made a serious decision to take matters further. A good Information Memorandum will help reduce staff unease by significantly reducing the number of clandestine meetings the Chairman has with people who are never heard of again.

For it to be useful, the Information Memorandum must inevitably contain a great deal of confidential information about your company. You may be reluctant to release such information, even to your intermediary. But a good intermediary will be able to produce an effective Information

Memorandum without divulging any potentially damaging information. It may be that fifteen per cent of your turnover is derived from one customer – an important fact to a potential purchaser which should be disclosed early – but the Information Memorandum does not have to name the customer.

All the information contained in the Memorandum must be approved by you for inclusion. The best way to achieve the balance between producing a meaningful Information Memorandum and not disclosing potentially damaging information is for you to provide all the information to the intermediary, for him to draft the memorandum, and for you to check the draft. Then no information will be disclosed to third parties without your explicit approval.

Although written up by the intermediary, virtually all the information must be provided by your company. A sample list of information required is set out in Appendix I. This list will vary for different types of business. Once this information is assembled, further points will be raised.

The Information Memorandum will also restate the profit history, adjusting for "personal" expenses and non-recurrent items. It would be preferable, however, that such expenses did not exist in the first place, rather than needing explanation to sceptical potential purchasers.

The intermediary will have his own format for the Information Memorandum. It must have clarity and be user friendly – surprisingly uncommon attributes. It should at the beginning have an "executive summary" explaining in brief terms what the business is and why it is an opportunity not to be missed.

The body of the Information Memorandum will have sections such as:-

History and Background
- How the business started
- Who started it
- Major developments
- Key influences
- The market place
- Unique Selling Points (USPs)
- Strengths and weaknesses
- Who owns it now
- Why it is up for sale

Sales
- Types of product
- Product sales profile
- Types of customers
- Customer sales profile
- Significant customers
- How customers are serviced
- Terms of business
- Competitors
- Sales structure
- Sales incentives
- Promotional activities

Operations
- Manufacturing process
- Buying process
- Components/raw material profile
- Supplier profile
- Stockholding policies
- Major items of plant and equipment

Premises
- Location
- Descriptions
- Activities at each location
- Lease details
- Valuations

Management and Staff
- Structure and organisation chart
- CVs for directors and senior management
- Skill requirements
- Awards or memberships
- Who would be leaving on a change of ownership
- Employment details for each category of staff:
  - pay levels
  - PRP
  - Share options
  - Holidays
  - Notice periods
  - Cars
  - Pensions
  - Insurances
  - Other benefits
  - Restrictive covenants

Financials
- Full actual historic
- Detailed forecasts
- Analysis of "true" profit history
- Description of extraordinary and exceptional items
- Explanation of unusual balance sheet items
- Details of possible synergistic savings
- Details of any assets or liabilities not being included in the sale

- Details of borrowings including HP, leasing and personal guarantees
- Details of any unusual or onerous agreements not mentioned elsewhere

Never forget that the Information Memorandum is a selling document.

Financial projections

The financial forecasts are probably the most important part of the Information Memorandum. It is what the potential purchasers are buying: the future. You may think you are selling the past results of your business, but no, those results only put into context your projections of what is going to happen in the future. A considerable part of the effort a potential purchaser will put into evaluating your business will be on scrutinising "the numbers". Therefore, too much thought and consideration cannot be applied in producing them.

A good intermediary will advise you on the format, detail and periods to be covered by the projections that are appropriate to your business. Indeed, a good intermediary should play devil's advocate to make sure the numbers stack-up and that the assumptions are realistic and robust.

Once a potential purchaser is satisfied with the overall feel of the prospective acquisition it is then that his accountants will examine and question in depth the forecasts. If, in their opinion, the forecasts look unreliable (or, as it is referred to in technospeak, rubbish) their interest will stop there and then. For you, this is a total waste of time and opportunity. Properly prepared and presented forecasts (which may well have given the same financial results) would have given them the confidence to proceed.

So what are the things to look out for? As a minimum there should be profit and loss accounts identifying the major sources of revenue and expenditure; detailed cashflow projections for the same periods and balance sheets which must tie together the profit and loss accounts and cashflow projections and reconcile back to the latest audited accounts. And, just as important as all the above combined, are the assumptions. It is the assumptions that tell whether the projections are viable, realistic, pessimistic, optimistic or codswollop. Assumptions are things that you don't know: but you must know why you think the assumption you have made is correct. You will be asked to explain and justify them.

A common mistake is to forget seasonality within the business and an even bigger mistake is to give a forecast that is like a dog's leg! It is very difficult for financial projections to have any credibility when they show good, steady historic growth and then, as soon as the business is for sale, lo and behold, the year after you depart sales are forecast to double and profits treble! Life (and business) is not like that. The effect of including such projections (apart from generating mild hilarity) is that it taints the whole of the Information Memorandum as wishful thinking and therefore something not to be taken seriously.

Some Information Memoranda include a "sensitivity analysis" in their financial projections, showing how the results vary if the principal assumptions are changed. Whilst this is useful when trying to raise funds, on the sale of a business it is probably more appropriate to let the prospective purchaser's accountants carry this out as part of their due diligence exercise.

Appendix III provides a set of sample financial projections, to show how they might appear in attachment to the Information Memorandum.

Confidentiality

Before the Information Memorandum is released to any potential purchaser, the intermediary should obtain specific clearance from you that that particular person may receive it.

The intermediary should obtain from the potential purchaser a written confidentiality undertaking, and also ensure that he has the financial ability to conclude the acquisition.

Sample information memorandum

A sample information memorandum is set out in Appendix II. This is provided for illustrative purposes only to give readers an idea of how the memorandum might look when presented to prospective purchasers. The actual contents and presentation of the memorandum will vary widely according to the particular characteristics and circumstances of the company in question.

5

Price

The best is the enemy of the good

You have been made an offer. It may not be what you had been hoping for, but it is nevertheless a good price. Only you can decide whether (a) to accept the offer; (b) to try to renegotiate; or (c) to keep the business on the market. And only you know the consequences of not accepting an offer in your own particular circumstances – whether of flourishing business, deteriorating business, your own age, failing health, pressure from the bank, family needs or whatever other reasons you have for selling.

The valuation of a business works on imperfect information. It is not like selling a house in a street of similar houses, in which case you know what the one down the road sold for a couple of months ago. There is no other business the same as yours in the same location and of similar size. Even if there were, how would you know its value?

There are no rules to tell you what your business is worth. There is no such thing as a "correct" price. A business can be worth twice as much to one person as to another – and neither will be wrong – or necessarily right for you. And note that if you have had a share valuation agreed by the Inland Revenue Share Valuation Division, do not think that that is even an approximation of the real value of your business. The valuation by the Share Valuation Division is merely a value agreed between them and your tax advisers based on a rigid set of rules used only for tax collection purposes. It has little to do with the best price that someone may be prepared to pay in the real world. Happily, an Inland Revenue agreed valuation is usually lower than an actual selling price.

There are in fact a number of different indicators used by the investment community for the purposes of valuation, as further referred to below, but remember that the purchaser is likely to have his own unique approach to valuing your business which will take into account his own preferences rather than any objective measure of valuation.

It is also worth noting that even the experts can get it wrong. For example, many companies have experienced financial problems in the 1990s through paying too much on acquisitions in the 1980s. Obviously neither the directors nor their highly-paid City advisers thought that they were paying too much at the time. On the other hand, Thorn EMI's £560m payment for the acquisition of Virgin Records in 1992 was lambasted by stockbroking analysts and the financial press for being far too high, but was amply justified by the subsequent results of the combined Group. Similarly, the Ladbroke Group's acquisition of Hilton Hotels in the 1980's was criticised only to be later roundly endorsed.

In the final analysis, however, risk is what the price is all about. A purchaser could put his money in a building society, earn interest on it and know it is guaranteed by the Bank of England. What makes an acquisition more viable is that it should produce a much better overall rate of return. The more risky a venture, the higher the rate of return that is required – otherwise no one would take on the additional risk. The corollary is that the higher the rate of return required, the lower the price will be. It is the assessment of the risk which will value your business. This assessment is not a science; it is an art.

At the end of the day it all boils down to a question of earnings, and the purchaser's required rate of return on capital invested in your business – and, of course, the premium he is prepared to pay (for whatever reason) for the privilege. This obviously makes it hard, if not impossible, to predict the outcome before embarking on the selling process, but here is a list of the considerations likely to affect the price you will ultimately receive:

Asset backing

Whilst few companies are valued by reference to their assets (with the obvious exception of property companies), the underlying asset value of a business nevertheless provides an important element of comfort (or otherwise) which will influence the price a purchaser may be prepared to pay. The more net assets a purchaser gets for his money, and the less debt within the company, the more attractive it will be.

One obvious implication of the asset value is that it defines the maximum downside for the purchaser – being the difference between what he is paying and the asset value of what he is acquiring.

A second important consideration is the accounting treatment of the "goodwill" arising on the acquisition (the difference between purchase price and asset value). This has either to be written off immediately, creating a dent in the assets of the acquirer, or written off over a number of years against the profits of the acquirer (such write-offs being non-tax deductible). Of course, this is more relevant to quoted companies than to private companies or individuals.

Finally, the availability of asset backing can be an important element in helping the purchaser put together his funding arrangements for the acquisition. For example, he may wish to factor the debts, or mortgage the freehold property to create cash. However, the technicalities of this must not contravene

S.151 of the Companies Act 1985 (which prevents a company own assets being used to provide financial assistance for the purchase of its own shares). Such a contravention could render the transaction invalid and illegal – your solicitor will safeguard you against this problem.

Barriers to entry

The more barriers to entry the better. The more difficult it is for others to get into your market and compete with you, the higher the value of your business. A barrier to entry could be large set-up costs, as for example in car manufacturing, or the need for international distribution centres and personnel. It could be a technical barrier, such as patents or the need for government licences, as with television franchises. It could be a physical limitation, such as "slots" at Heathrow airport. It could be market dominance. Whatever the barriers to entry, they give an element of security to a potential purchaser, and also prevent him thinking that he could start up an equally profitable competitive operation at a lower net cost than the price you want for your business.

Break-up value

This is the value that would be left, net of tax, if the business were closed down, the assets sold and the creditors paid off. This value rarely has anything to do with the net asset value as shown in your audited accounts. Usually the break-up value is lower, as your accounts will be prepared on a "going concern" basis which ignores the redundancy costs of closing a business and the discount on the stock value if it were sold as a job lot. Leasehold premises may also need to be written down to create a "negative value" if a premium has to be paid to the landlord to cancel the lease.

Sometimes the break-up value can be higher than the value shown in the accounts. This can occur where assets (such as freehold land or major items of plant and machinery) are shown in the accounts at their historic cost less depreciation, whereas their market value is now significantly higher. In the 1960s and 1970s in particular, Jim Slater and others made their fortunes by recognising that some businesses were under-performing and that the true value of the underlying assets bore no relationship to the figures shown in the audited accounts. They bought the companies, closed many of them down and sold off their assets, often at a vast profit. This technique is known as "asset-stripping". If you unknowingly sell a business for less than its break-up value, you have been very badly advised.

Cash flow

Businesses generating cash are more desirable than cash-hungry businesses for three obvious reasons. First, cash-hungry businesses require ongoing funding. Second, there is an inbuilt uncertainty with these businesses concerning the point at which they may start to yield distributable surpluses. And third, in the case of cash-generating businesses, these have the significant advantage of being able to assist in the repayment of any financing costs relating to the acquisition.

Some businesses require extra cash in order to grow, while others produce excess cash as they grow. A good example of the former is leasing companies: the profit margins are generally not large, and therefore retained profits cannot produce the funds necessary to generate very much new business. To produce a further £100 of profit may require, for example a further £1500 to be invested (though naturally the leases eventually become cash-positive). An example of a "cash cow" is exhibition-organising companies, which generate cash as exhibitors pay in advance: therefore, as more exhibitions are organised (i.e. the business is expanding), more exhibitors pay in advance, generating more cash.

Some acquirers will actually use the cash flow projections to provide a basis for valuation, using a method known as "discounted cash flow" (DCF) analysis. This is a technique designed to discount the projected stream of cash flows at the investor's required rate of return (the "discount rate"), to calculate their "net present value". This approach is popular among business schools and certain sections of the financial community. It is more commonly used for project evaluation than company valuation but can nevertheless provide a useful indicator of underlying value in a business.

One criticism is that it does not recognise the premium certain buyers will pay for a business.

Dependency

If your business is heavily dependent on something or someone, then its profits are at risk. The dependency could be, for example, the personal loyalty shown by major customers or suppliers to the Chairman. This will probably cause serious problems if the Chairman is to leave the company at or shortly after the sale. The dependency could be on a supplier who accounts for (say) eighty per cent of purchases; if the supplier were to go bust, or have an irresolvable altercation with your company, production and credit terms could be badly affected. The situation is mirrored by dependency on one customer, or a small number of customers. Dependency could also be on a niche, which, although it might have been there for decades and even be protected by patents or legislation, can still disappear. An example of such a business would have been the supplier of the drinking vessels used by the Royal Navy to dispense their tots of rum! Dependency could be the utilisation of a specific process or market place. Traditional typesetters have declined sharply since the widespread use of computers which allow originators to send a disk (or even transmit copy down the telephone line) direct to printers.

Every business must in some sense be dependent. It is the degree of dependency that matters, along with the purchaser's perception of its risk. If your business is highly dependent, you will already be fully conversant with this type of risk as you will have been living under the Sword of Damocles, perhaps for many years.

Earn-out

In most circumstances you will get more money for your business if you are prepared to stay a while to ensure a smooth hand-over and to be paid (in part) at an agreed multiple of future profits. Nothing could seem simpler – but now part of the risk has been transferred to you. In nearly all earn-out situations some money will be paid on completion, but usually a substantial part is paid in the future – perhaps up to five years hence. All manner of awful things could happen during this time that will affect how much money you finally receive. You must evaluate the risk of more jam tomorrow against a smaller amount now.

A good corporate solicitor will as far as possible have a watertight agreement to protect your rights and allow you to maximise the earn-out payment. However, rarely is any thought given to what happens if, through ill-health or death, you cannot earn your money. A discussion with a good insurance broker is always worthwhile if you are considering accepting an earn-out.

No matter how legally watertight the earn-out agreement is, if the purchaser is unscrupulous and wants to ignore it there is little you can do but resort to litigation, where most victories are Pyrrhic. Your opponents will generally have more time and money than you, and will probably drag matters out to debilitate you financially. Choose your purchaser carefully.

The other major downside to earn-outs is what might happen if the acquirer goes bust. In such circumstances you could end up with nothing. It is possible, however, (although uncommon) to have a legal charge over the shares you have sold, so that you get them back if you don't receive all the money due to you.

For the above reasons, many people will not consider an earn-out except for a small part of the total price. In reality, however, the overwhelming majority of earn-outs do work properly.

The upside is that the acquirer may be prepared to pay considerably more on a deferred basis and you will have the opportunity to benefit from any additional growth he brings to the business.

Form of consideration

Subject to tax planning, there is no substitute for one hundred per cent cash on the table. However, as referred to in the previous section, most purchasers are less aggressive about price if there is an element of deferred consideration; for example, loan notes with deferred encashment dates. Also attractive to quoted companies is acceptance of their shares, which you agree to hold for a minimum period and which may have deferred dividend rights.

Again, you need to assess the risks against the rewards.

Industry norms

In some industries there are generally accepted methods of valuation. For example, in the security guard business it is common to value an acquisition as a percentage of turnover. A few years ago, before their bubble burst, Body Shop franchises had a standard minimum price. The usual price factors as discussed in this chapter had only a small effect.

If the normal industry valuation produces a lower value than could otherwise be reasonably expected for a business in a different industry, it would be wise to approach buyers who are not in the industry and therefore not wedded to this form of valuation.

Interest rates

Other things being equal, the higher prevailing interest rates, the lower the value of a company, and vice versa. The theory is that extra profit is required from a business to match the higher return offered by putting the money on deposit (or the cost of borrowing the money to finance the purchase). In practice, interest rates have very little direct effect on valuations. This is because vendors will generally not accept a lower price simply on account of high interest rates and will if necessary wait a couple of years until there is a change in the economic cycle.

Management

Good quality management is always of value. From the purchaser's perspective, having continuity of good managers causes less disruption to the business in terms of customer and supplier relationships, and less apprehension with the staff. It makes the whole transaction less risky as the new owner has the benefit of their experience to fall back on. Good remaining management also gives the impression that what is being bought is a real business rather than an empire based on one man.

Obligations

The majority of obligations come in two forms: leases and employee costs. Where a business has commitments, it can (a) affect the ability of new owners to make changes and (b) create long-term demands on the business which have to be met even though they are no longer relevant to the current business.

Property leases (which only a decade ago were considered assets) can, in the current climate, be extremely difficult to dispose of. If the lease has "upwards only" rent reviews, the cost of moving premises could be huge. The current rent (at the inflated rate) will already have been taken into account in assessing current profits – but the sting in the tail is that to move, your business would, in one way or another, have to subsidise another business's occupation of your old premises for the duration of the lease. A lease can also represent a commitment under hire-purchase or lease-purchase agreements. Some capital equipment, such as a £1m printing press, create a very big commitment to fund each month.

Employee costs are not only the cost of terminating long-term contracts with senior executives. They are also the potential redundancy costs accruing to an ageing and long-standing workforce. In a sluggish manufacturing business, the redundancy costs of moving production to another town can be several times the amount paid for the whole company.

Other obligations can include minimum royalty payments for the purchase of a patent, or the granting of exclusive selling rights for a region or country.

Order book

The best time to sell is when the order book is full. This will give a lot of comfort to a potential purchaser. It is astounding how many otherwise logical, calculating businessmen react to a low order book by deciding to sell. And if you have already decided to sell, don't let the business run down before you do so. Work extra hard and attract orders, then if you still want to sell, fine. If you can't increase the order book, how can you expect anyone to pay a premium price for your business?

Price-Earnings ratios ("P/E")

There is a lot of nonsense talked about Price Earnings Ratios, especially in relation to private companies.

A P/E ratio is calculated by taking the latest reported post tax profits of a company and comparing them against the value of the company. In publicly quoted companies it is easy to calculate the P/E as the published accounts of a quoted company are required to show the amount of (post-tax) earnings per share. This gives you the "E" of the "P/E". The "P" is the price per share, and this can be easily ascertained from *The Financial Times*, other quality newspapers, etc. Many newspapers, including *The Financial Times*, show the P/E as well as the price of each share. In a private company the P/E is derived by dividing the value of the company (e.g. the offer from a purchaser) by the post-tax profit for the year. So a P/E of, say, ten means that the value of the company is equal to ten times last year's post-tax profits.

A quick glance down the share prices pages of *The Financial Times* shows that some companies have P/Es of six or seven whilst others are in the 70's and 80's. Why such a huge disparity? The reason is simple: the "E" is based on past results while the "P" is the current share price, reflecting anticipation of *future* earnings. High P/Es reflect an expectation of rapid profit growth; low P/Es reflect an assumption of stagnant or even declining profits.

Whilst P/Es can give a rough guide to the valuation levels applicable to different industry sectors, and different kinds of company within each sector, remember that in each specific case the P/E is affected daily by particular announcements or events relating to the company concerned. In any event the price investors will pay for a quoted investment where they can realise their investment at a moment's notice is obviously much higher than the price they might be prepared to pay for a share of an unlisted company.

There are many different kinds of P/E, in addition to the normal calculation referred to above, depending on the earnings figure used in the calculation: "prospective P/Es" relate price to anticipated future earnings; "fully diluted P/Es" adjust the earnings to allow for dilution if the company may have a commitment to issue some shares in the future or has done so part way through the previous year; "fully taxed P/Es" adjust the earnings to assume taxation at the normal rate if the company has benefited from a lower tax rate; "pre-tax P/Es" are calculated using pre-tax earnings as the name suggests. So, when in negotiations with prospective purchasers, and, having made sure which type of P/E you are dealing with you must also make sure that it is based on the appropriate "E"arnings. In many private businesses there is expenditure that would not be incurred if the purchaser owned it. This must be adjusted for.

For the most part, P/Es quoted for public companies give a fair approximation of that company's value although of course share prices often become volatile when a company is the subject of a takeover bid, or other speculation. In private companies it is a totally different ball game. The true profit a business is making is only really known to the vendor and the purchaser. Also, deals involving allegedly high P/Es for private companies are usually dependent on some earn-out and therefore at the time of the deal the actual P/E cannot be known by anyone. Add to this the boastful disposition of some vendors and the information disseminated via the traditional industry grapevine or trade press, and a totally misleading impression of company values is created.

The Financial Times gives a summary of the average P/Es for each industry sector. Probably the only relevance this has to sellers of private businesses is that private companies invariably sell at a significant discount to their quoted counterparts.

Potential

Potential is clearly a major influence on price. A growing company in a growing market is clearly worth more than a company with the same profits but which is declining in a declining industry. Potential could be there because of the growth that would occur from being part of a larger group – such as wider distribution, shared technological developments, and cost cutting. For each different type of purchaser a good intermediary will detail the additional benefits that would accrue from the acquisition. The purchaser will, of course, be fully aware of these benefits – it is for the intermediary to inform the purchaser that you also know them and that this must be reflected in the price.

Notwithstanding synergistic gains, the full inherent potential of the business must be demonstrated in the Information Memorandum. The most effective method of doing this is to include detailed profit and loss and cash flow projections (see page 41). This can mean a lot of work, especially if your business is not used to producing them, but even only the promise of "more jam tomorrow" can only have a positive effect on the selling price.

Profit history

If profits have been volatile in the past, there will obviously be concern that they may be volatile again in the future. Purchasers will inevitably discount the current and forecast profit levels if there is a hint that the profits are either not consistent or not maintainable.

Purchaser

Choosing the right customers is as important for a successful business as is choosing the right suppliers. Choosing the right purchaser is no different.

Quoted companies can issue shares to finance an acquisition. The shares can, by prior arrangement, be simultaneously sold to raise the cash to pay you. The prior arrangement is usually called a "vendor placing" and should in practice be invisible to you. A similar technique as far as you are concerned is called a "rights issue". The advantage for quoted companies in being able to issue shares for acquisitions is that, other things being equal, if a company has a higher P/E ratio than it is paying for the acquisition, and if this P/E continues to be applied to the combined earnings, there is an automatic uplift in the value of the whole company which benefits the shareholders (and the value of the directors' share options). In effect the market ascribes a value to the acquired business higher than the price actually paid. The bigger the difference in the P/E's between the buying and selling companies, then the bigger the increase in value to the acquirer's shareholders. It follows that when paying a premium for your business the purchaser's shareholders are still better off than by not doing a deal at all, providing the P/E paid is below theirs. Therefore if you are negotiating with a quoted company, it is easy to ascertain whether they can pay more by checking their P/E, which will be quoted daily in *The Financial Times*.

Acquisitive quoted companies can be on a treadmill of needing to make acquisitions to justify their high P/E ratio. This is fine for you, selling the business, so long as you don't have to take the highly rated shares and hold them until the steam inevitably runs out. A classic line from the Chairman is, "Look, I know we are only paying you this amount, but take our shares and in eighteen months' time they will be worth double – just look at our track record!" If you find yourself on the receiving end of this, then ask the Chairman to guarantee the arrangement personally. It will soon become evident whether he has as much faith in his company as he is asking you to have! Quoted companies sometimes "have" to make an acquisition to mask their own shortcomings. If they are aware that their results are going to be below market expectations – resulting in a significant fall in the share price and therefore the threat of a takeover (and the directors being ousted) – they need to "buy" profits with an acquisition. Taking shares in such a company is not advisable.

Where a purchaser is borrowing the money, you need to be circumspect. Firstly, the deal might not go through because he may not have the wherewithal to borrow the money; secondly, you may end up negotiating with the funders as well as the purchaser – all supposedly on the same side but with different criteria. This all takes a lot more time and money (not least in increased legal costs) and you will not get an over-generous deal because (a) the funders (particularly venture capital firms) will not allow an excessive price to be paid no matter how keen the front man is, and (b) interest will have to be paid on the borrowed money putting an additional strain on profits and cash flows.

Having said that, many deals are done using borrowings to finance them, but a decisive, financially able purchaser will generally mean a smooth progression to a satisfactory deal for both sides and can save substantially on your legal costs.

The third aspect to choosing the right purchaser, as alluded to elsewhere in this book, is that of finding one who can add substantially to the value of your company, perhaps by cutting out several hundred thousand pounds in costs which are duplicated in his business – such as the accounts department, premises, or the sales director. A purchaser will not pay you for all the added value he will generate, but he may share some of it with you as it is in his interest to do the deal.

Quality of earnings

If Company A makes the same profit each year as Company B, it might seem logical to assume that the companies have the same value. This ignores the "quality" of those profits. If company A has five-year cleaning contracts with (say) government departments, then a prospective purchaser knows that the company he is buying has a secure future. Without taking on any new business, it will survive in the short term, is not readily open to predatory attacks from the competition and is not dependent on key staff staying with the company. Company B, on the other hand, is a graphic design company whose order book is never more than four weeks' sales. Customers may be fickle, going elsewhere without warning. If one or two key staff left (or lost their creative thrust) they would be difficult to replace and even more difficult to go into competition with. In this scenario, would you be prepared to pay the same for each company?

Quality of earnings is also linked to dependency (see page 50).

Quality of earnings is really a comfort factor for purchasers. The effect, though, is very real. This is why, traditionally, quoted property companies have on average, a higher P/E ratio than builders' merchants.

Size

Generally, the larger and more established a business is, the higher its P/E ratio. This is simply because the business is less vulnerable to attack; it will have a better infrastructure, and is therefore safer. It is also true that it is easier to raise £10m of funding for an acquisition than it is to raise £250k for equally viable propositions.

There is, strangely, a psychological aspect to pricing. No matter how good the profits are, buyers will rarely pay more than the turnover for a business.

Whilst many of the above factors are obvious, and some overlap, it does not necessarily follow that the absence of certain advantages will deter all purchasers or affect the price. For example, it could be that a purchaser wants to capitalise on your distribution network but close down your factory and move production to his own works – in this case he would be delighted if there were no senior management staying on, who would be expensive to dismiss.

The purchaser interested in the rum-tot vessels company might have (as his hidden agenda) the plan to shift production to giftwares, and therefore the only effect the Royal Navy dependency has is on the price negotiations with you. The moral of this story is that if your business has a "downside", it does not have to affect the price unless you let it.

It is always surprising to see how much a purchaser will pay for a business he really wants.

6

Vendor Politics

If you live long enough you will see everything

"Vendor politics" is a horrible piece of jargon. It means that the vendor has got his act together and is prepared to negotiate seriously for the sale of his business. What could be simpler? You want to sell and someone else wants to buy. However, the reality can be so different. The purchaser is about to spend a considerable sum on accountancy, due diligence, legal fees (it is the purchaser's solicitor who prepares the Sale and Purchase Agreement), tax advice and the opportunity cost of working on the acquisition of your business. Therefore, before doing so the purchaser will make sure that the vendor really does want to sell and that negotiations can be undertaken in a timely and professional manner. If a purchaser is not convinced of your determination to conclude a deal, he may well decide that he should pursue other opportunities, or he may ask you to indemnify him for his professional costs. In the former instance you may have lost the opportunity of getting the best deal; in the latter instance you may be happy to proceed on this basis, but if something totally outside your control happens before you and he have signed on the bottom line – his solicitor may find a fault in your title to the freehold premises; you have a major fire in your warehouse; you have a heart-attack – then you will have to pick up the bill for his professional fees at a time when you need extra expenses like you need a hole in the head. These extra costs are unlikely to be allowed against tax, and you will certainly not be able to recover the VAT.

Having a professional intermediary who is fully prepared shows that you are serious about selling. It also gives the purchaser a degree of comfort that negotiations are unlikely to founder because of an unforeseen technicality. Thirdly, and perhaps most significantly, it enables you to take a tough line without being confrontational – this is of particular importance if you will continue to work in the business under the new ownership, either for transitional purposes or perhaps as part of an earn-out arrangement.

It is possible to have detailed negotiations running with two or more interested parties. At first glance, this may appear an attractive method of keeping your options open and thereby securing the best price. If you do try and keep too many balls in the air there is a fair to middling chance you will drop them all. The reality is that if you are running with several prospective purchasers it probably means that you are not at all convinced that you will actually conclude a deal with any of them. There is also the waste of an amazing amount of management time and resource that is needed to have detailed negotiations with several interested purchasers. It is probably better that you stop dealing with all of them and find a really suitable purchaser – this of course may mean that you change your advisers.

Apart from all this there are real commercial concerns about divulging extremely confidential information and giving access to key staff to several purchasers, some of whom may be competitors. What happens to the value of your business if negotiations break down or you proceed with someone else and detailed information about your business is then commonly known? Should one of the parties become aware that you are in detailed negotiations with someone else they may perceive that you have been acting in bad faith in allowing them to incur substantial professional costs without informing them of the possible risk that you will sell to someone else. This may well cause them to act in bad faith towards your business and "unfairly" use the information they have gleaned.

From a practical point of view, once basic terms have been agreed, a purchaser will invariably want a lock-out or exclusivity period. It is of course down to you to decide if that is what you want but if it is not raised then you should be wary about the ability of the purchaser and his professional advisers.

Moving to the tactical aspects of negotiation, there are many ways to deal with potential purchasers. It is for you to decide what is right for you in your circumstances.

On price, one ploy is not to meet anyone until they have submitted an indicative offer price, based on the Information Memorandum, for your consideration. This way you will (a) avoid wasting time meeting purchasers who would not have met your price expectations, and (b) have a "ball park" figure on which to negotiate. This technique can work, but it eliminates purchasers who do not want to commit themselves to price at such an early stage. It also lends itself very well to the negotiation technique of "offer the seller what he wants, then as new facts come to light (as they invariably do during due diligence investigations, etc.) take things away from the offer until you end up paying what you want". This approach is used widely, though surreptitiously and with cunning.

In any event, allow potential purchasers to visit your premises only the minimum number of times. This implies to a potential purchaser that there are several others negotiating to buy the business, and stops him gleaning further confidential information when he may not in the end be the actual purchaser. Also, strangers have a very disturbing effect on staff, and there are no guarantees that a potential purchaser will become the actual purchaser.

When negotiating on price, there is a golden rule: "He who speaks first loses". Break this rule at your financial peril. You cannot possibly know what the potential purchaser wants to do with your business and therefore how much he is prepared to pay. Be laid back when talking of price – he must make the first move. Beyond this small piece of advice, it would take another whole book on the art of negotiating to impart anything else that is so important.

You should be aware that most of the concessions that you will make (even on price) occur in the presence of solicitors during the long and laborious discussions over the Sale and Purchase Agreement (see next chapter). So be on your guard. You will have great difficulty winning every negotiation point – just make sure you win the important ones. Never forget why you are selling and what you want to achieve.

From a negotiating stance, your absence during the detailed negotiations is very effective, providing you are not concerned if one particular buyer withdraws from the deal. By being absent, perhaps abroad (see "Taxation", page 69), you stop any of the coercion that usually occurs after several hours around a lawyer's conference room table, with each side trying to complete a deal. Indeed, using this trick, the purchasers will often give way to your nominated representative on a particular point at issue in order to progress matters as they know that he will have to contact you for instructions (which can take several days) unless they relent. This approach may lead to slightly higher legal costs, but it does prevent you from being manipulated during the lengthy negotiations over the Sale and Purchase Agreement and allow you time to reflect on the bigger issues. It also allows you to stonewall on an issue without their having any means of appeal – therefore if they really want to do the deal, they will give in.

If you have a minimum price below which you will not sell, and the potential purchaser wants to negotiate on that price, do not be drawn into trying to justify it. You will be open to attack on the basis of your calculations, and are bound to be the loser.

You have nothing to gain by having to justify the price you want. It is for the potential purchaser to try to justify to himself that the price is acceptable. If he can do this, he will pay; if he can't do it, he won't pay – it's as simple as that.

You can sometimes feel unsure of a potential purchaser. His offer may be the highest, or the most suitable for what you are trying to achieve, but you may have doubts about his seriousness, or about his financial ability. An acid test is to ask him to indemnify you against (reasonable) legal costs should he withdraw from the transaction. He may ask you to reciprocate, and indemnify him should you withdraw, but at least you will be more comfortable in incurring legal costs if you have security that the potential purchaser is acting in good faith.

Should you have meetings at the purchaser's premises, do not sign the visitors' book. All nosy salesmen read them when signing in, so this would be tantamount to an announcement to the industry that you were "in talks" about selling your business. Similarly, when you have potential purchasers known within the industry visiting your premises, remove the signing-in book.

Once the terms have been agreed, professional advisers like having Heads of Agreement prepared before proceeding to either due diligence or the Sale and Purchase Agreement. The advantages are that the Heads of Agreement set out in simple outline what has been agreed between you and the purchaser, and thus should avoid any misunderstanding between the parties. The Heads of Agreement also act as the starting point for briefing each party's lawyers. All this is true, but in practice the actual deal often bears little resemblance to the Heads of Agreement, which can require considerable extra up-front work. Do not be misled into believing that the Heads of Agreement are always binding, even if they explicitly state that they are and everyone signs as such. In reality, so much changes on both sides that it can be impossible to sue on the original document, even if it has been drafted by solicitors.

7

TAXATION

It's not what you earn – it's how much you keep

The good news is that all taxation on the sale of a business is voluntary! If you really don't want to pay tax on the sale proceeds, then you don't have to. Some tax planning may of course be necessary, and some of the inconvenience may not be considered to be worthwhile – even to save £1,000,000.

By far the simplest method of saving tax is to emigrate. This may not be as drastic as it first appears. After a life of hard work, what could be difficult about living in the South of France, or even Jersey? You would need to leave the UK before you decided to enter into an agreement to sell your business, and before 6 April of the tax year in which you actually sell it. You may also have to sell your home so that you don't have a place of residence in the UK. By emigrating you are not banished from the UK. You can return to the UK for limited periods and you can even return permanently but only after a sufficient lapse of time, but with substantially enhanced wealth.

If short-term emigration is not for you, then another way to save tax is to sell your company for shares or loan notes in the acquiring company. Tax is payable only when the shares are finally sold or the loan stock encashed (this can be piecemeal, and utilise the annual capital gains tax exemption – currently £6,800). If you hold them until your death, they will totally escape capital gains tax. They will form part of your estate for inheritance tax – but so would the cash, on which you would also already have paid capital gains tax. It can be risky to take shares in any company, and to have virtually your entire wealth locked into one company is a very high-risk strategy. If financial security is not high on your agenda, you don't need the ready cash and you are impressed with how good a deal the management of the acquiring company did with you, then consider taking shares. If you are worried about security, loan notes may be safer but you should consider whether they can be secured, preferably guaranteed by a bank. Interest could be paid to you quarterly or half-yearly, and the notes could be secured against the acquiring company's assets so that if things do go wrong, you get your money before anyone else, even before the Inland Revenue and Customs and Excise. If all you intend to do with your sale proceeds is "stick it in the building society", then this route gives you an (agreed) fixed rate of interest, and this is calculated on the gross sale proceeds rather than on the after-tax sale proceeds you would have in the building society. The rate of interest itself would probably also be higher, reflecting the acquirer's marginal cost of capital, and if held until death also avoid capital gains tax. Purchasers, too, are attracted to these forms of paying for acquisitions, as there is no immediate outflow of cash or placing costs and they may therefore be prepared to pay you more for your business.

Still not happy? Then, within three years, roll over the taxable capital gain part of the proceeds (not necessarily the whole proceeds) into ordinary shares in an unquoted trading company. There are certain restrictions on the types of trade that can be undertaken – these are listed in Appendix VI. But it could still be a fairly passive business activity to keep you mildly occupied during retirement. It could be a company belonging to an old friend in which you effectively become partners, or you could set your son or daughter up in business. If you, your family or current business partners control less than 30% of the shares the first £150,000 of investment should be eligible for Enterprise Investment Scheme relief which incredibly produces a negative tax rate of 20% – you actually get a rebate from the Inland Revenue.

If none of the above is suitable and you do prefer to pay tax, all is not lost.

The calculation of the taxable capital gain on the disposal of a business (including shares in a family trading company) has, since the 1998 Budget, become extremely complex as the former Indexation and Retirement Relief provisions are being replaced by "Taper Relief" and there are 5 years of transitional arrangements.

Basically, the taxable capital gain is calculated as the difference between the sale price (net of costs) and the original cost (or March 1982 value if higher and owned then) adjusted for inflation up to April 1998 and then reduced by the appropriate amount of Retirement Relief (applicable if you are over 50) and then further reduced by the relevant taper relief percentage depending on the timing of the disposal and if owned on 17th March 1998. You may wish to read this paragraph again!

Appendix VII shows the different amounts of tax payable by an individual who makes £1m of gains, depending in which year the gain is made. The table shows how expensive it can be for individuals who are eligible for Retirement Relief to postpone the sale. Although called Retirement Relief – you don't actually have to retire to be eligible. The relief is still available if you sell-out and remain employed by the business or start-up another business.

If your wife works in the business (she does not have to be a director), and is over 50, you should seriously consider transferring enough shares into her name to maximise her relief. The transfer of shares should be separated by as long a period as possible from the actual sale, or the Inland Revenue may disallow it as a tax avoidance arrangement. The sale or gift of shares between husband and wife is exempt from tax.

If, for whatever reason, you don't want your wife to have shares in your business, or she is not old enough to qualify for retirement relief, then there might be a good case for sacking her! Providing her contract of employment does not bind you to make severance payments, the first £30,000 of an ex-gratia payment could be tax free.

Pre-sale pension contributions can also be used as a tax-free way to acquire some benefits for you and your wife.

Another option is for you and your wife to become consultants (involving very little actual work) for the new owners for, say, five years at £27,000 per annum plus inflation. This way, providing you have no other taxable income, you could draw a total of £270,000 of the sale proceeds with an effective tax rate of twenty-one per cent.

All the above are simple outlines of tax-saving opportunities. They are examples of only some of the things that can be achieved to maximise your return for the years of hard work (and family suffering) that have gone into building your business. Although it is a long established tenet of English law that a person may organise their affairs to minimise tax, it is also well established that artificial transactions solely for the purpose of reducing tax are ineffective. As with all tax advice, it needs to be considered with your specific circumstances, and therefore professional advice must be sought before taking any action.

It is also important to realise that the above tax saving opportunities will not exist forever. It is very dangerous to plan for future years using the tax laws as they are now. The current Government has declared a policy of eliminating any transactions that are done solely to avoid tax.

Should you, for whatever reason, decide to pay capital gains tax, it becomes due for payment on the 31 January following the 5 April after the deal (and for tax purposes, the deal is treated as being the date of formally entering the agreement – not the date when you get the money), so if negotiations are taking place in February or March, it is as well to consider actually signing the agreement after 5 April.

8

The Sale and Purchase Agreement

The main purpose of English law is to make more work for itself

The Sale and Purchase Agreement is a horrendous document. It is probably the most important piece of paper you will ever sign, and yet there will be large parts that you won't understand. It is full of awful jargon, and some of the phrases, in Latin as well as English, you will never come across again and will probably never want to.

So it will come to pass that your solicitor and their solicitor will want you to sign and take responsibility for a document half an inch thick and on which, to a great extent, your future prosperity depends.

Some businessmen take the approach, "I trust my solicitor, but if anything does go wrong I can always sue him". This attitude can seem to work because things do not usually go wrong, but if they do and you want to sue your solicitor over a document you yourself signed (and you now haven't got any money anyway) – forget it. It is far better to understand what the risks are in the first place and to make your own assessment.

For insomniacs and serious sellers, an example of a Sale and Purchase Agreement is included as Appendix V. This example is not definitive. There are so many variations on how an acquisition can be structured that no one example could cover every situation.

In theory, everything in a Sale and Purchase Agreement is "by agreement", and therefore negotiable. In practice, if you did try to negotiate everything the result would probably be legal costs greater than the price you are getting for your business.

Solicitors are professionals. For their own satisfaction and edification (as well as to keep their professional indemnity insurance down), they will want to do a good job for you – at any price! Well-intentioned solicitors frequently argue at length over obscure clauses in the Sale and Purchase Agreement, trying to protect their respective clients. You and the purchaser should be aware of this highly remunerative tendency and be prepared to intervene.

The principle behind the Sale and Purchase Agreement is straightforward: it details who is buying what from whom, for how much and when. What could be simpler? It is not even necessary to have a written agreement. Some acquisitions occur simply by the vendor handing over a signed share transfer form and his share certificates in exchange for a cheque. This method of executing the transaction does, however, leave the purchaser exposed, so the purchaser's solicitor will want safeguards for his client and want them documented. For this reason it is the purchaser's solicitor who usually prepares the Sale and Purchase Agreement. And, as you will not know whether any of the safeguards being requested in the incomprehensible (draft) document are reasonable, you will have to consult a solicitor. What may have started out as a simple deal – in essence no different from the types of deal you have done all your business life – transmogrifies into an expensive, intellectually esoteric bun fight between two highly paid solicitors. Instead of being in control of your destiny, without realising it you find yourself being led round and round the mulberry bush and told what you must and must not do. You have been warned.

Do consider agreeing a fixed fee with your solicitor before he is appointed. He or she will not like it, but it will help procure an expedient transaction.

Sale and Purchase Agreements with quoted companies tend to be lengthier, as the purchase may be subject to obtaining shareholder approval at a specially convened meeting or, even more complicated, subject to a successful placing of shares to pay for the acquisition. Usually, both of these requirements are formalities – but they are formalities which have to be fully documented.

Obviously, the Sale and Purchase Agreement should be a record of the agreement you have with the purchaser. The initial agreement between the two parties will be refined and modified by the time an engrossed Sale and Purchase Agreement is produced. You must never lose sight of the basic terms of the agreement, and the fact that they are indeed recorded in the Sale and Purchase Agreement. This may seem trite, but after many days of many hours in a solicitor's office it can be very easy to lose sight of the wood for the trees.

Of the other points in the Sale and Purchase Agreement:

Interpretation

This section tries to explain the definition of terms that appear in the rest of the Agreement. Many of the definitions are obvious (e.g. Purchaser's Solicitors), but be careful: whenever any of the defined terms are used in the document, they mean the precise wording attributed to them and not what they may mean in normal usage.

Do not be overly concerned about references to various sections of Taxes Acts or Companies Acts; this is an area you can leave to your solicitor.

Warranties and Disclosure Letter

The concept of giving warranties is very simple: you are explicitly guaranteeing certain facts about your business. Warranties apportion financial risk away from the purchaser (*caveat emptor*) to the seller. They are therefore safeguards for the Purchaser.

However, the warranties in the Sale and Purchase Agreement, which are drawn up by the purchaser's solicitor, will contain statements about your business that you have never made, or indeed that may not be true. It is your responsibility to go through each warranty, with your solicitor, and if it is not accurate state the correct position in a Disclosure Letter. This, therefore, is a very important document. It is your safeguard that there are no repercussions on you if, in the future, there are problems with the company concerning the information in the warranties.

The warranties are the basis of the safeguards the purchaser's solicitor uses to protect his client. Each individual warranty is there for a reason; fail to understand any of them at your peril.

It is a matter for negotiation as to which warranties you will or will not accept and what your Disclosure Letter may contain. In many instances the warranties are used to "flush out" any bad news about the company before the legally binding contract is signed. It can occur that a matter (say, specific litigation) is known of by both sides, but the purchasers do not allow it to be formally disclosed so that if it does cause loss to the company, then the amount of that loss will be down to you.

There is usually a minimum aggregate amount (which can vary from £1000 upwards) below which any loss to the company will not be recovered from you. There is also usually a maximum that can be recovered, which is very rarely greater than the price the purchaser is paying.

It is worth noting that over sixty per cent of a Sale and Purchase Agreement is usually devoted to warranties and indemnities.

Indemnities

Some matters are better dealt with as warranties, others as indemnities. Generally, warranties shift the responsibility for any loss to the company on to the vendor. The redress for such loss is usually damages awarded by a Court. To claim under a warranty the common law imposes a duty to establish and assess the loss and for such losses to be mitigated (i.e. to take all steps necessary to reduce the amount of the loss). Indemnities, however, shift responsibility purely and simply on a pound-for-pound basis, without the need to mitigate the loss. If a certain events happens (such as litigation from a former employee) you pay; there is no discussion. Indemnities are much more effective at parting you from your money.

Earn-outs

If your deal contains an earn-out provision do make sure that the wording of the appropriate clauses will work in practice. You know how your business works and what can affect it – your solicitor does not.

Earn-outs vary in length from a couple of months (to the end of the current financial year) to several years. For tax as well as commercial reasons the purchaser will want a limit on the maximum amount payable to you under the earn-out, so do not limit your potential upside by being too realistic if you are ever asked early in discussions what is the maximum profit the business could achieve in the next couple of years.

If the acquirer is a quoted company they will need to show continual improving profits so it may be possible to obtain an undertaking in the Sale and Purchase Agreement that they will do what they can to improve the profitability of the business during the earn-out period.

There are generally two ways to protect the future profits of the business you have sold so that you can maximise your earn-out. The simplest way is that you are allowed, unfettered, to manage the business for the period of the earn-out. Any dealings with the new owner (or associated companies) will be solely at your discretion. Whilst this can be appropriate it may hinder the reasons why the purchaser wants the business. The other method is whereby the purchaser runs the business but you have the ability to veto anything they do. In reality it does not stop them from doing what they want but the effects of such actions will be "added back" in the earn-out calculation.

In any case, it is always better for your auditors to continue in office until the expiration of the earn-out period and for them to do the calculation of the earn-out rather than the acquirer's auditors.

Completion

The completion section sets out what each party to the transaction has to do at the "completion meeting" in order for you to receive your banker's draft. If any of the requirements are not met it can scupper the deal. In complex transactions, rehearsal completion meetings are held to try to eliminate last-minute hitches.

At the completion meeting, the Sale and Purchase Agreement and stock transfer forms are signed. There are usually a series of directors' and shareholders' meetings involving resignation and appointment of directors, company secretary, auditors, change of registered office, bank mandates and possibly a new Memorandum and Articles of Association. Fortunately, all this is orchestrated by the solicitors.

Restrictive covenants

Depending on the nature of the deal, it is usual for the vendors to agree that they will not compete against their old company for a specific period of time – often three to five years. The restrictions may have geographical limitations, and include current customers and even the poaching of staff. So do not think that you will get a large slug of money to fund you setting-up in direct competition.

Restrictive covenants are a continually changing area of the law so your solicitor will not be able to give you absolute advice but generally speaking the tougher the restrictions are the better it is for you: they are more likely to be unenforceable.

9

How to Live Happily Ever After

Let MacIntyre & Co look after all your financial needs

MacIntyre & Co is a medium sized firm of Chartered Accountants based in the City of London. The firm's success can be attributed to its desire to excel in its chosen business areas and to pioneer new financial developments. There are a number of distinctive features:-

Technical Excellence

The firm has established a reputation for excellence through the publication of numerous books and articles. Specialist sectors include family owned businesses, professional and other partnerships, Trade Associations, charities, trusts and high net worth individuals. Many of the firm's clients operate internationally.

Tax Consultancy

MacIntyre & Co are well known for providing innovative solutions for both individual and corporate clients. We provide tax consultancy to both UK and overseas clients.

Personal Financial Planning

MacIntyre & Co can help in assessing your personal financial planning requirements. We work with professional IFAs in order to provide a balanced and appropriate solution.

Quasi Finance Director

A business which is too small to need a full-time finance director can rent as much of one as they need from MacIntyre & Co.

Corporate Finance

MacIntyre & Co provides a mini-merchant banking service for small to medium size businesses, raising equity and other forms of finance and arranging mergers, acquisitions and disposals. MacIntyre & Co were one of the pioneers of smaller management buyouts in the UK.

Trusts

MacIntyre & Co have a dedicated department providing services to all types of trust. We also have an offshore trust company based in Jersey.

Charities and Not for Profit Organisations

MacIntyre & Co's charity department provides specialist audit, accountancy and tax services to a large variety of charitable and not for profit organisations. The firm is particularly well known for its expertise in the educational sector, acting for many of the country's best known schools.

International

MacIntyre & Co is the co-founder of MacIntyre Sträter International Limited (MSI), a global network of independent professional firms incorporating accountants, lawyers, tax advisers, offshore service providers and specialist members. This unique network offers clients the availability of professional advice from approximately two hundred member firms in more than 75 countries. It is sixteenth largest of such firms in the world.

Appendix I

Checklist of Information Required to Prepare an Information Memorandum

Accounts

- Statutory accounts and detailed profit and loss accounts for each of the last five financial years, plus explanation of any exceptional or extraordinary matters for the company and each of its subsidiaries

- For each of the last five years, details of any income or expenditure not directly related to trading, e.g. wives' cars charged to the business, excessive pension contributions, etc.

- Latest management accounts

- Any budgets and cash flow projections prepared for the business (see Chapter 4)

Sales

- Details of any customer who accounts for more than five per cent of the turnover in the current and previous financial years

- Copies of any sales/agency agreements with third parties

- Copies of all promotion material, including advertisements

- Copy of the aged debtors' listing

Purchases

- Details of any supplier who accounts for more than ten per cent of purchases in the current and previous financial years

- Copies of any supplier agreements

- Copy of the aged creditors' report

Production

- A description of each of the processes, and in particular any distinguishing abilities of the business

- A listing of major items of plant and equipment with the date of acquisition, original cost, net book value, current market value and replacement cost

- An analysis of turnover for the current and previous financial years between:

  - Bought-in components
  - Manufactured components
  - Bought-in complete products

Directors and staff

- An organisation chart, including names and job titles

- For directors, executives and key personnel, a schedule of names, ages, job descriptions, lengths of service, salaries and any benefits, including cars and pensions

- Details of those who would be leaving the company on a change of ownership

- A brief career resume for each director and senior executive

- Details of any long-term Consultants

Assets

- Details of freehold properties and current market valuations

- Details of leasehold properties and copies of the leases

- Details of trademarks, trade names, copyrights or other intellectual property of the company or its subsidiaries

- Details of investments

- Details of any assets or liabilities which may not form part of the Sale

Sundry

- A copy of the bank facility letter

- Details of pension commitments

- Details of any onerous or other agreements not made in the ordinary course of business

- Details of awards or membership of associations

Appendix II

Good Business Limited

Information Memorandum (sample)

Contents

Disclaimer
1. Background and History
2. Sales
3. Operations
4. Management and Staff
5. Financial

Appendices
I   Organisation Chart
II   Major Items of Plant & Equipment
III Market Sector Activities
IV   Audited Accounts for the Year Ended 30th April 1998
V   Financial Projections for the Three Years Ending 30th April 2001
VI   ISO 9002 Certificate
VII Promotional Literature

Disclaimer

The purpose of this Information Memorandum is to assist the recipient in deciding whether to investigate the possibility of acquiring Good Business Limited ("Good Business"). The Information Memorandum is not intended to form the basis of any acquisition decision. Each recipient must make its own independent assessment in order to determine its interest in acquiring Good Business and should obtain independent professional advice.

The information in this Information Memorandum has been supplied by the management of Good Business and has not been independently verified by MacIntyre Corporate Finance Limited. Neither MacIntyre Corporate Finance Limited nor Good Business nor any of their respective officers, agents or employees give or have any authority to give any representation or warranty (express or implied) for the accuracy and completeness of this Information Memorandum or any other written or oral communication transmitted or made available to a prospective purchaser, nor shall they be liable in any way for any inaccuracy, omission or misleading statement herein. Only those particular formal representations which may be made to the purchaser in a formal agreement as and when it is finally executed, and subject to such limitations and restrictions as may be specified therein, shall have any legal effect.

This Information Memorandum has been delivered to interested parties for information purposes only and upon the express understanding that such parties will use it for the purposes set out above. In furnishing this Information Memorandum, MacIntyre Corporate Finance Limited and Good Business undertake no obligation to provide the recipient with access to any additional information or to update this Information Memorandum or to correct any inaccuracies therein which may become apparent and reserve the right, without advance notice, to change the procedure for the acquisition or to terminate negotiations at any time prior to the signing of any binding agreement for the acquisition. In no circumstances will MacIntyre Corporate Finance Limited or Good Business be responsible for any costs or expenses incurred in connection with any preparation and submission of preliminary purchase proposals or for any other costs and expenses incurred by potential purchasers in connection with the proposed acquisition.

All enquiries and communications of whatever nature regarding the proposed sale should be directed only to Gary Morley or Guy Rigby at the following address:-

MacIntyre Corporate Finance Limited
28 Ely Place
London EC1N 6RL

Tel: 0171 430 0000
Fax: 0171 404 9709
Email: GCMORLEY@COMPUSERVE.COM

Under no circumstances should prospective purchasers make contact with the owners, management, employees, customers, suppliers or other professional advisers of the business until invited to do so by MacIntyre Corporate Finance Limited.

1. Background and History

1.1 Good Business Limited is a highly successful manufacturer and distributor of shu-shu valves to the film production industry. Currently approximately half of the company's sales are from their own production. The balance are imported.

1.2 Good Business was founded in Coventry in 1948 by Sydney James. It was acquired in 1973 by the current owner and managing director, Jim Dale.

1.3 The business moved to the present 20,000 sq.ft. site in Leicester in 1982.

1.4 Jim Dale with his wife are the only directors of the company. Mrs. Dale is not involved with the management of the company.

1.5 The current shareholdings are:-

Jim Dale	78%
Mrs. Dale	18%
Barbara Windsor (Mr. Dale's sister)	4%
	100%

1.6 Mr. Dale is now 69 and wishes to retire. The whole of the shares in the company are offered for sale.

1.7 Mr. Dale would be happy to remain with the company for an agreed period to ensure a smooth handover to a new owner.

1.8 It is anticipated that the recent favourable tax breaks available to films produced in the UK will have a favourable effect on the company's business.

2. Sales

2.1 Shu-shu valves are consumable products used in the film production business. They are sold both direct to film production companies and also to film equipment hire companies for re-sale. All of the company's sales are in the UK.

2.2   An example of the company's promotional literature is attached as Appendix VII.

2.3   Approximately one-third of sales are direct to film production companies. The selling price to the hire companies is approximately 25% lower than for direct sales.

2.4   Approximately 3% of total sales are returned from the film production companies for full credit. There is no such return policy for the film equipment hire companies.

2.5   The company has approximately sixty film equipment hire companies as customers. This is approximately one-third of the market.

2.6   None of the film equipment hire companies accounts for more than 5% of the company's sales.

2.7   The average order value is approximately £10,000.

2.8   An analysis of market sector activities is shown in Appendix III.

2.9   The company employs a sales manager and a salesman, both of whom spend substantially the whole amount of their time out of the office.

2.10   The sales manager; Kenneth Williams (age 48), has been with the company for ten years. The salesman; Charles Hawtree (age 31), has been with the company for three years.

2.11   There is a certain amount of technical input needed for each sale. The salesman advises on the best type of shu-shu valve required and approximate quantity needed depending on the type of film production e.g. comedy, action, erotic, musical.

2.12 The company advertises extensively in trade magazines as well as sponsoring several technical awards at national industry events.

2.13 Good Business is the only UK based manufacturer of shu-shu valves, the competition being mainly US manufacturers who import direct to the film equipment hire companies.

3. Operations

3.1 The company operates from one site in Leicester.

3.2 The general manager; Frankie Howerd (age 51), has direct responsibility for buying, production and stock control.

3.3 The company manufactures the two most commonly used types of shu-shu valve: in line and polarised.

3.4 The flanges and balls are machined and tooled in house. The plastic bearings and cowlings manufacturing is sub-contracted. All assembly is carried out on site.

3.5 The company employs eight tongue and groovers and has five apprentices.

3.6 The premises are split approximately:-

Office accommodation	7,000 sq.ft.
Warehousing and distribution	5,000 sq.ft.
Manufacturing and assembly	8,000 sq.ft.
	20,000 sq.ft.

3.7 There is a sophisticated computerised stock control/production management system which integrates into the company's management information system and financial accounts.

3.8 Orders are received approximately three months ahead of delivery, enabling the company to have a relatively low stockholding requirement.

3.9 The company is ISO 9002 registered.

3.10 A list of major items of plant and equipment is attached as Appendix II.

4. Management and Staff

4.1 Attached as Appendix I is the organisation chart of the company. The company currently employs 41 staff.

4.2 Jim Dale is the chairman of the company. Since 1997 he has worked three days a week.

4.3 There is a management committee which comprises:-

Sales Manager   Charles Hawtree
General Manager   Frankie Howerd
Administration Manager   Hattie Jacques

Apart from strategic decisions, all day to day operations of the business are decided upon by the management committee which meets weekly.

4.4 Ms. Jacques, when required, also acts as Mr. Dale's personal assistant.

4.5 The accounts department, which consists of a purchase ledger clerk, a sales ledger clerk and a part-time payroll clerk, all report to Hattie Jacques.

4.6 Apart from the directors, there is no pension scheme. Mr. Dale's remuneration package reflects his ownership of the company.

5. Financial

5.1 Attached as Appendix IV are the audited accounts for the year ended 30th April 1998.

5.2 Attached as Appendix V are the financial projections for the three years ending 30th April 2001.

5.3 Summary

£'000	Actual			Forecast		
	1996	1997	1998	1999	2000	2001
Sales	3,384	3,678	3,965	4,201	4,453	4,717
Gross profit	900	990	1,135	1,288	1,399	1,504
Gross margin	26.6%	26.9%	28.6%	30.7%	31.4%	31.9%
Overheads	566	598	633	686	751	816
Operating profit	334	392	502	602	648	688
Mr. Dales's costs inc. in the above	130	137	140	156	158	165
Interest	(44)	(23)	(9)	4	18	31
Restated profit before tax	420	506	633	762	824	884

5.4 All expenditure on research and development is written off in the year it is incurred.

5.5 The freehold of the property is owned by Mr. Dale's pension fund. It is available on short or long lease or is for sale depending on the requirements of the purchaser.

5.6 Included in motor vehicles is a 1973 Jensen Interceptor MK111 with a WDV of £1. This would be removed from the company at book value and excluded from the sale of the company.

APPENDICES (to be added as attachments)

I   Organisation Chart
II   Major Items of Plant & Equipment
III   Market Sector Activities
IV   Audited Accounts for the Year Ended 30th April 1998
V   Financial Projections for the Three Years Ended 30th April 2001 (see page 99)
VI   ISO 9002 Certificate
VII   Promotional Literature

Appendix III

Good Business Limited

Financial Projections
To 30th April 2001

Good Business Limited

Annual Profit Summaries for the
Five Years Ending 30th April 2001

	Actual 1997 £	Sales %	Actual 1998 £	Annual Increase %	1999 £	Annual Increase %	2000 £	Annual Increase %	2001 £	Annual Increase %
Sales										
Factored	1,772,718	48.2%	1,805,987	1.9%	1,842,722	2.0%	1,873,933	1.7%	1,905,790	1.7%
Manufactured	1,905,089	51.8%	2,158,688	13.3%	2,357,988	9.2%	2,578,929	9.4%	2,811,032	9.0%
	3,677,807		3,964,675	7.8%	4,200,710	6.0%	4,452,862	6.0%	4,716,822	5.9%
Cost of Sales										
Purchases	960,625	26.1%	989,943	3.1%	1,031,694	4.2%	1,079,819	4.7%	1,132,037	4.8%
Consumables	146,261	4.0%	157,176	7.5%	166,768	6.1%	176,779	6.0%	187,258	5.9%
Repairs & Renewals	37,999	1.0%	40,202	5.8%	37,367	-7.1%	39,235	5.0%	41,001	4.5%
Power	87,012	2.4%	93,729	7.7%	97,954	4.5%	102,852	5.0%	108,508	5.5%
Plant Hire	16,795	0.5%	18,645	11.0%	17,854	-4.2%	18,747	5.0%	19,778	5.5%
Transport	95,897	2.6%	98,844	3.1%	98,946	0.1%	103,893	5.0%	110,127	6.0%
Subcontractors	563,120	15.3%	600,901	6.7%	600,180	-0.1%	630,189	5.0%	671,151	6.5%
Direct labour	764,204	20.8%	816,459	6.8%	848,295	3.9%	878,209	3.5%	903,055	2.8%
Depreciation	15,399	0.4%	14,045	-8.8%	14,000	-0.3%	23,600	68.6%	39,600	67.8%
	2,687,312	73.1%	2,829,944	5.3%	2,913,058	2.9%	3,053,322	4.8%	3,212,516	5.2%
Gross Profit	990,495		1,134,731	14.6%	1,287,651	13.5%	1,399,540	8.7%	1,504,306	7.5%
Margin	26.9%		28.6%		30.7%		31.4%		31.9%	
Establishment Costs										
Light & Heat	31,543	0.9%	32,481	3.0%	33,475	3.1%	35,149	5.0%	36,906	5.0%
Rent & Rates	87,159	2.4%	91,702	5.2%	99,417	8.4%	104,388	5.0%	123,178	18.0%
Insurance	24,021	0.7%	24,957	3.9%	25,139	0.7%	26,396	5.0%	27,980	6.0%
Repairs	3,575	0.1%	2,759	-22.8%	3,650	32.3%	3,833	5.0%	4,043	5.6%
	146,298	4.0%	151,899	3.8%	161,681	6.4%	169,765	5.0%	192,107	13.2%
Administration Expenses										
Directors' Remuneration	93,670	2.5%	93,670	0.0%	104,497	11.6%	104,496	0.0%	110,766	6.0%
Directors' Expenses	23,232	0.6%	26,155	12.6%	27,762	6.1%	30,000	8.1%	30,000	0.0%
Directors' Pensions	20,000	0.5%	20,000	0.0%	24,000	20.0%	24,000	0.0%	24,000	0.0%
	136,902	3.7%	139,825	2.1%	156,259	11.8%	158,496	1.4%	164,766	4.0%
Printing & Stationery	3,659	0.1%	4,011	9.6%	4,236	5.6%	4,380	3.4%	4,643	6.0%
Postage	938	0.0%	998	6.4%	1,201	20.3%	1,260	4.9%	1,336	6.0%
Sundry Expenses	8,508	0.2%	9,104	7.0%	9,659	6.1%	9,840	1.9%	10,430	6.0%
Telephone	2,873	0.1%	3,176	10.5%	4,244	33.6%	4,380	3.2%	4,643	6.0%
Office Wages	108,236	2.9%	118,875	9.8%	130,849	10.1%	136,200	4.1%	145,734	7.0%
Staff Welfare	3,989	0.1%	4,059	1.8%	4,205	3.6%	4,380	4.2%	4,643	6.0%
Audit & Accountancy	4,980	0.1%	5,100	2.4%	5,400	5.9%	5,640	4.4%	6,000	6.4%
Legal & Professional	4,282	0.1%	6,878	60.6%	5,120	-25.6%	5,400	5.5%	5,700	5.6%
Bank Charges	2,841	0.1%	3,151	10.9%	3,302	4.8%	3,480	5.4%	3,720	6.9%
Depreciation	1,612	0.0%	1,612	0.0%	1,800	11.7%	1,920	6.7%	2,035	6.0%
	278,820	7.6%	296,789	6.4%	326,275	9.9%	335,376	2.8%	353,649	5.4%
Operating Profit	391,656	10.6%	501,542	28.1%	601,531	19.9%	647,679	7.7%	687,924	6.2%
Interest (Paid)/Received	(22,783)	-0.6%	(8,840)	-61.2%	3,568	-140.4%	18,085	407.1%	30,555	69.0%
Profit Before Tax	£368,873	10.0%	£492,702	33.6%	£605,099	22.8%	£665,763	10.0%	£718,479	7.9%
Corporation Tax	81,152	2.2%	108,394	33.6%	133,122	22.8%	96,468	-27.5%	108,065	12.0%
Dividends	100,000	2.7%	120,000	20.0%	200,000	66.7%	250,000	25.0%	300,000	20.0%
Retained Profit	£187,721	5.1%	£264,308	40.8%	£271,977	2.9%	£319,295	17.4%	£310,413	-2.8%

Good Business Limited

Profit Forecast for the Year Ending 30th April 1999

	Actual 3 months to July £	August £	Sept £	October £	Nov £	December £	Jan £	Feb £	March £	April £
Sales										
Factored	553,247	184,211	221,053	202,632	165,790	55,263	73,684	110,526	128,947	147,369
Manufactured	710,909	235,297	282,356	258,827	211,767	70,589	94,119	141,178	164,708	188,238
	1,264,156	419,508	503,409	461,458	377,557	125,852	167,803	251,705	293,655	335,606
Cost of Sales										
Purchases	310,477	103,031	123,637	113,334	92,728	30,909	41,212	61,819	72,122	82,425
Consumables	50,187	16,654	19,985	18,320	14,989	4,996	6,662	9,993	11,658	13,324
Repairs & Renewals	10,367	3,000	3,000	3,000	3,000	3,000	3,000	3,000	3,000	3,000
Power	24,540	10,488	12,585	11,536	9,439	3,146	4,195	6,293	7,341	8,390
Plant Hire	4,354	1,500	1,500	1,500	1,500	1,500	1,500	1,500	1,500	1,500
Transport	25,532	10,488	12,585	11,536	9,439	3,146	4,195	6,293	7,341	8,390
Subcontractors	159,697	62,926	75,511	69,219	56,634	18,878	25,170	37,756	44,048	50,341
Direct labour	212,301	70,666	70,666	70,666	70,666	70,666	70,666	70,666	70,666	70,666
Depreciation	3,200	1,200	1,200	1,200	1,200	1,200	1,200	1,200	1,200	1,200
	800,655	279,953	320,670	300,312	259,594	137,442	157,801	198,518	218,877	239,236
Gross Profit	463,501	139,555	182,739	161,147	117,963	(11,590)	10,002	53,186	74,778	96,370
Margin	36.7%	33.3%	36.3%	34.9%	31.2%	-9.2%	6.0%	21.1%	25.5%	28.7%
Establishment Costs										
Light & Heat	8,455	2,780	2,780	2,780	2,780	2,780	2,780	2,780	2,780	2,780
Rent & Rates	30,567	7,650	7,650	7,650	7,650	7,650	7,650	7,650	7,650	7,650
Insurance	6,239	2,100	2,100	2,100	2,100	2,100	2,100	2,100	2,100	2,100
Repairs	950	300	300	300	300	300	300	300	300	300
	46,211	12,830	12,830	12,830	12,830	12,830	12,830	12,830	12,830	12,830
Selling Costs										
Advertising & Sponsorship	18,759	6,250	6,250	6,250	6,250	6,250	6,250	6,250	6,250	6,250
Travelling & Entertainment	211	600	600	600	600	600	600	600	600	600
Motor Expenses	4,605	1,250	1,250	1,250	1,250	1,250	1,250	1,250	1,250	1,250
Salesmen's Wages	14,946	4,900	4,900	4,900	4,900	4,900	4,900	4,900	4,900	4,900
Commissions	6,943	2,300	2,300	2,300	2,300	2,300	2,300	2,300	2,300	2,300
Depreciation	3,750	1,250	1,250	1,250	1,250	1,250	1,250	1,250	1,250	1,250
	49,214	16,550	16,550	16,550	16,550	16,550	16,550	16,550	16,550	16,550
Administration Expenses										
Directors' Remuneration	26,125	8,708	8,708	8,708	8,708	8,708	8,708	8,708	8,708	8,708
Directors' Expenses	7,062	2,300	2,300	2,300	2,300	2,300	2,300	2,300	2,300	2,300
Directors' Pensions	6,000	2,000	2,000	2,000	2,000	2,000	2,000	2,000	2,000	2,000
	39,187	13,008	13,008	13,008	13,008	13,008	13,008	13,008	13,008	13,008
Printing & Stationery	1,086	350	350	350	350	350	350	350	350	350
Postage	301	100	100	100	100	100	100	100	100	100
Sundry Expenses	2,639	780	780	780	780	780	780	780	780	780
Telephone	1,094	350	350	350	350	350	350	350	350	350
Office Wages	32,749	10,900	10,900	10,900	10,900	10,900	10,900	10,900	10,900	10,900
Staff Welfare	1,055	350	350	350	350	350	350	350	350	350
Audit & Accountancy	1,350	450	450	450	450	450	450	450	450	450
Legal & Professional	1,295	425	425	425	425	425	425	425	425	425
Bank Charges	827	275	275	275	275	275	275	275	275	275
Depreciation	450	150	150	150	150	150	150	150	150	150
	82,033	27,138	27,138	27,138	27,138	27,138	27,138	27,138	27,138	27,138
Operating Profit	286,043	83,037	126,221	104,629	61,445	(68,108)	(46,516)	(3,332)	18,260	39,852
Interest Received	(751)	(102)	328	1,030	1,356	1,582	511	(288)	(182)	82
Profit Before Tax	£285,292	£82,935	£126,549	£105,658	£62,801	(£66,525)	(£46,004)	(£3,619)	£18,079	£39,935

Sample Financial Projections

Good Business Limited

page 4

Profit Forecast for the Year Ending 30th April 2001

	May £	June £	July £	August £	Sept £	October £	Nov £	December £	Jan £	Feb £	March £	April £	Total £
Sales													
Factored	187,667	191,110	189,389	191,089	229,307	210,198	171,980	57,327	76,436	114,653	133,762	152,871	1,905,790
Manufactured	276,194	281,262	278,728	282,121	338,545	310,333	253,909	84,636	112,848	169,273	197,485	225,697	2,811,032
	463,861	472,373	468,117	473,210	567,852	520,531	425,889	141,963	189,284	283,926	331,247	378,568	4,716,822
Cost of Sales													
Purchases	111,327	113,369	112,348	113,570	136,285	124,927	102,213	34,071	45,428	68,142	79,499	90,856	1,132,037
Consumables	18,415	18,753	18,584	18,786	22,544	20,665	16,908	5,636	7,515	11,272	13,151	15,029	187,258
Repairs & Renewals	3,417	3,417	3,417	3,417	3,417	3,417	3,417	3,417	3,417	3,417	3,417	3,417	41,001
Power	9,042	9,042	9,042	9,042	9,042	9,042	9,042	9,042	9,042	9,042	9,042	9,042	108,508
Plant Hire	1,648	1,648	1,648	1,648	1,648	1,648	1,648	1,648	1,648	1,648	1,648	1,648	19,778
Transport	9,177	9,177	9,177	9,177	9,177	9,177	9,177	9,177	9,177	9,177	9,177	9,177	110,127
Subcontractors	55,929	55,929	55,929	55,929	55,929	55,929	55,929	55,929	55,929	55,929	55,929	55,929	671,151
Direct labour	75,255	75,255	75,255	75,255	75,255	75,255	75,255	75,255	75,255	75,255	75,255	75,255	903,055
Depreciation	3,300	3,300	3,300	3,300	3,300	3,300	3,300	3,300	3,300	3,300	3,300	3,300	39,600
	287,510	289,891	288,701	290,125	316,597	303,361	276,890	197,475	210,711	237,183	250,418	263,654	3,212,516
Gross Profit	176,351	182,482	179,416	183,085	251,256	217,170	149,000	(55,512)	(21,427)	46,744	80,829	114,914	1,504,306
Margin	38.0%	38.6%	38.3%	38.7%	44.2%	41.7%	0	-39.1%	-11.3%	16.5%	24.4%	30.4%	31.9%
Establishment Costs													
Light & Heat	3,076	3,076	3,076	3,076	3,076	3,076	3,076	3,076	3,076	3,076	3,076	3,076	36,906
Rent & Rates	10,265	10,265	10,265	10,265	10,265	10,265	10,265	10,265	10,265	10,265	10,265	10,265	123,178
Insurance	2,332	2,332	2,332	2,332	2,332	2,332	2,332	2,332	2,332	2,332	2,332	2,332	27,980
Repairs	337	337	337	337	337	337	337	337	337	337	337	337	4,043
	16,009	16,009	16,009	16,009	16,009	16,009	16,009	16,009	16,009	16,009	16,009	16,009	192,107
Selling Costs													
Advertising & Spons.	7,155	7,155	7,155	7,155	7,155	7,155	7,155	7,155	7,155	7,155	7,155	7,155	85,860
Travelling/Entertainmt	642	642	642	642	642	642	642	642	642	642	642	642	7,704
Motor Expenses	1,855	1,855	1,855	1,855	1,855	1,855	1,855	1,855	1,855	1,855	1,855	1,855	22,260
Salesmen's Wages	7,875	7,875	7,875	7,875	7,875	7,875	7,875	7,875	7,875	7,875	7,875	7,875	94,500
Commissions	2,675	2,675	2,675	2,675	2,675	2,675	2,675	2,675	2,675	2,675	2,675	2,675	32,100
Depreciation	2,350	2,350	2,350	2,350	2,350	2,350	2,350	2,350	2,350	2,350	2,350	2,350	28,200
	22,552	22,552	22,552	22,552	22,552	22,552	22,552	22,552	22,552	22,552	22,552	22,552	270,624
Administration Expenses													
Directors' Remunerat.	9,230	9,230	9,230	9,230	9,230	9,230	9,230	9,230	9,230	9,230	9,230	9,230	110,766
Directors' Expenses	2,500	2,500	2,500	2,500	2,500	2,500	2,500	2,500	2,500	2,500	2,500	2,500	30,000
Directors' Pensions	2,000	2,000	2,000	2,000	2,000	2,000	2,000	2,000	2,000	2,000	2,000	2,000	24,000
	13,730	13,730	13,730	13,730	13,730	13,730	13,730	13,730	13,730	13,730	13,730	13,730	164,766
Printing & Stationery	387	387	387	387	387	387	387	387	387	387	387	387	4,643
Postage	111	111	111	111	111	111	111	111	111	111	111	111	1,336
Sundry Expenses	869	869	869	869	869	869	869	869	869	869	869	869	10,430
Telephone	387	387	387	387	387	387	387	387	387	387	387	387	4,643
Office Wages	12,145	12,145	12,145	12,145	12,145	12,145	12,145	12,145	12,145	12,145	12,145	12,145	145,734
Staff Welfare	387	387	387	387	387	387	387	387	387	387	387	387	4,643
Audit & Accountancy	500	500	500	500	500	500	500	500	500	500	500	500	6,000
Legal & Professional	475	475	475	475	475	475	475	475	475	475	475	475	5,700
Bank Charges	310	310	310	310	310	310	310	310	310	310	310	310	3,720
Depreciation	170	170	170	170	170	170	170	170	170	170	170	170	2,035
	29,471	29,471	29,471	29,471	29,471	29,471	29,471	29,471	29,471	29,471	29,471	29,471	353,649
Operating Profit	108,319	114,450	111,384	115,053	183,224	149,138	80,968	(123,544)	(89,459)	(21,288)	12,797	46,882	687,924
Interest Received	728	1,213	2,007	2,190	2,727	3,579	4,003	4,443	2,967	2,185	2,112	2,400	30,555
Profit Before Tax	£109,047	£115,663	£113,391	£117,243	£185,951	£152,717	£84,971	(£119,101)	(£86,492)	(£19,103)	£14,909	£49,282	£718,479

Good Business Limited

Profit Forecast for the Year Ending 30th April 2000

	May £	June £	July £	August £	Sept £	October £	Nov £	December £	Jan £	Feb £	March £	April £	Total £
Sales													
Factored	184,530	187,916	186,223	187,895	225,474	206,684	169,105	56,368	75,158	112,737	131,526	150,316	1,873,933
Manufactured	253,389	258,039	255,714	258,827	310,592	284,709	232,944	77,648	103,531	155,296	181,179	207,061	2,578,929
	437,919	445,955	441,937	446,722	536,066	491,394	402,049	134,016	178,689	268,033	312,705	357,377	4,452,862
Cost of Sales													
Purchases	106,195	108,144	107,170	108,330	129,996	119,163	97,497	32,499	43,332	64,998	75,831	86,664	1,079,819
Consumables	17,385	17,704	17,545	17,735	21,282	19,508	15,961	5,320	7,094	10,641	12,414	14,188	176,779
Repairs & Renewals	3,270	3,270	3,270	3,270	3,270	3,270	3,270	3,270	3,270	3,270	3,270	3,270	39,235
Power	8,571	8,571	8,571	8,571	8,571	8,571	8,571	8,571	8,571	8,571	8,571	8,571	102,852
Plant Hire	1,562	1,562	1,562	1,562	1,562	1,562	1,562	1,562	1,562	1,562	1,562	1,562	18,747
Transport	8,658	8,658	8,658	8,658	8,658	8,658	8,658	8,658	8,658	8,658	8,658	8,658	103,893
Subcontractors	52,516	52,516	52,516	52,516	52,516	52,516	52,516	52,516	52,516	52,516	52,516	52,516	630,189
Direct labour	74,226	74,226	74,226	74,226	74,226	74,226	74,226	74,226	74,226	70,059	70,059	70,059	878,209
Depreciation	1,300	1,300	1,300	1,300	1,300	1,300	1,300	1,300	3,300	3,300	3,300	3,300	23,600
	273,683	275,950	274,817	276,167	301,380	288,773	263,560	187,922	202,528	223,574	236,181	248,787	3,053,322
Gross Profit	164,236	170,004	167,120	170,555	234,686	202,620	138,489	(53,905)	(23,839)	44,459	76,525	108,590	1,399,540
Margin	37.5%	38.1%	37.8%	38.2%	43.8%	41.2%	0	-40.2%	-13.3%	16.6%	24.5%	30.4%	31.4%
Establishment Costs													
Light & Heat	2,929	2,929	2,929	2,929	2,929	2,929	2,929	2,929	2,929	2,929	2,929	2,929	35,149
Rent & Rates	8,699	8,699	8,699	8,699	8,699	8,699	8,699	8,699	8,699	8,699	8,699	8,699	104,388
Insurance	2,200	2,200	2,200	2,200	2,200	2,200	2,200	2,200	2,200	2,200	2,200	2,200	26,396
Repairs	319	319	319	319	319	319	319	319	319	319	319	319	3,833
	14,147	14,147	14,147	14,147	14,147	14,147	14,147	14,147	14,147	14,147	14,147	14,147	169,765
Selling Costs													
Advertising & Spons.	6,750	6,750	6,750	6,750	6,750	6,750	6,750	6,750	6,750	6,750	6,750	6,750	81,000
Travelling/Entertainmt	600	600	600	600	600	600	600	600	600	600	600	600	7,200
Motor Expenses	1,750	1,750	1,750	1,750	1,750	1,750	1,750	1,750	1,750	1,750	1,750	1,750	21,000
Salesmen's Wages	7,360	7,360	7,360	7,360	7,360	7,360	7,360	7,360	7,360	7,360	7,360	7,360	88,320
Commissions	2,500	2,500	2,500	2,500	2,500	2,500	2,500	2,500	2,500	2,500	2,500	2,500	30,000
Depreciation	1,600	1,600	1,600	1,600	1,600	1,600	1,600	1,600	1,600	1,600	1,600	1,600	19,200
	20,560	20,560	20,560	20,560	20,560	20,560	20,560	20,560	20,560	20,560	20,560	20,560	246,720
Administration Expenses													
Directors' Remunerat.	8,708	8,708	8,708	8,708	8,708	8,708	8,708	8,708	8,708	8,708	8,708	8,708	104,496
Directors' Expenses	2,500	2,500	2,500	2,500	2,500	2,500	2,500	2,500	2,500	2,500	2,500	2,500	30,000
Directors' Pensions	2,000	2,000	2,000	2,000	2,000	2,000	2,000	2,000	2,000	2,000	2,000	2,000	24,000
	13,208	13,208	13,208	13,208	13,208	13,208	13,208	13,208	13,208	13,208	13,208	13,208	158,496
Printing & Stationery	365	365	365	365	365	365	365	365	365	365	365	365	4,380
Postage	105	105	105	105	105	105	105	105	105	105	105	105	1,260
Sundry Expenses	820	820	820	820	820	820	820	820	820	820	820	820	9,840
Telephone	365	365	365	365	365	365	365	365	365	365	365	365	4,380
Office Wages	11,350	11,350	11,350	11,350	11,350	11,350	11,350	11,350	11,350	11,350	11,350	11,350	136,200
Staff Welfare	365	365	365	365	365	365	365	365	365	365	365	365	4,380
Audit & Accountancy	470	470	470	470	470	470	470	470	470	470	470	470	5,640
Legal & Professional	450	450	450	450	450	450	450	450	450	450	450	450	5,400
Bank Charges	290	290	290	290	290	290	290	290	290	290	290	290	3,480
Depreciation	160	160	160	160	160	160	160	160	160	160	160	160	1,920
	27,948	27,948	27,948	27,948	27,948	27,948	27,948	27,948	27,948	27,948	27,948	27,948	335,376
Operating Profit	101,581	107,349	104,465	107,900	172,031	139,965	75,834	(116,560)	(86,495)	(18,196)	13,870	45,935	647,679
Interest Received	76	558	1,288	1,445	1,945	2,730	3,115	3,522	1,371	629	568	837	18,085
Profit Before Tax	£101,658	£107,907	£105,753	£109,344	£173,976	£142,696	£78,949	(£113,039)	(£85,123)	(£17,567)	£14,438	£46,773	£665,763

Appendix 3

Good Business Limited

Annual Balance Sheet Forecasts
As At 30 April

	Actual 1997 £	Actual 1998 £	1999 £	2000 £	2001 £
Fixed Assets					
Plant & Equipment	238,936	267,796	267,796	492,796	492,796
Fixtures, Fittings etc	10,624	11,294	11,294	11,294	11,294
Motor Vehicles	59,770	59,770	59,770	59,770	77,770
	309,330	338,860	338,860	563,860	581,860
Accumulated Depreciation	95,265	125,866	156,666	201,386	271,221
	214,065	212,994	182,194	362,474	310,639
Current Assets					
Stocks & WIP	384,939	465,380	470,493	475,718	362,349
Trade Debtors	806,232	873,228	981,212	1,017,985	1,053,778
Prepayments	37,312	39,116	39,116	39,116	39,116
Bank Account	0	0	22,437	228,999	656,301
	1,228,483	1,377,724	1,513,258	1,761,818	2,111,544
Current Liabilities					
Trade Creditors	457,966	425,689	273,704	338,540	259,427
Accruals	18,135	18,342	18,642	18,882	19,242
Corporation Tax	61,152	83,394	103,122	96,468	108,065
Proposed Dividend	100,000	120,000	200,000	250,000	300,000
Bank Overdraft	247,783	113,840	0	0	0
VAT	67,832	73,129	71,683	72,806	77,439
PAYE & NIC	34,370	36,706	36,706	36,706	36,706
	987,238	871,100	703,857	813,402	800,879
Net Current Assets	241,245	506,624	809,401	948,416	1,310,665
Assets Employed	455,310	719,618	991,595	1,310,890	1,621,303
Shareholders Funds					
Share Capital	20,000	20,000	20,000	20,000	20,000
Reserves	247,589	435,310	699,618	971,595	1,290,890
Profit & Loss A/c	187,721	264,308	271,977	319,295	310,413
	455,310	719,618	991,595	1,310,890	1,621,303

Sample Financial Projections

Good Business Limited

Monthly Balance Sheet Forecasts for the Year Ending 30th April 1999

	July	August	Sept	October	Nov	December	Jan	Feb	March	April
	£	£	£	£	£	£	£	£	£	£
Fixed Assets										
Plant & Equipment	267,796	267,796	267,796	267,796	267,796	267,796	267,796	267,796	267,796	267,796
Fixtures, Fittings etc	11,294	11,294	11,294	11,294	11,294	11,294	11,294	11,294	11,294	11,294
Motor Vehicles	59,770	59,770	59,770	59,770	59,770	59,770	59,770	59,770	59,770	59,770
	338,860	338,860	338,860	338,860	338,860	338,860	338,860	338,860	338,860	338,860
Accumulated Depreciation	133,266	135,866	138,466	141,066	143,666	146,266	148,866	151,466	154,066	156,666
	205,594	202,994	200,394	197,794	195,194	192,594	189,994	187,394	184,794	182,194
Current Assets										
Stocks & WIP	485,986	475,683	455,077	393,258	403,561	424,168	434,471	444,774	468,544	470,493
Trade Debtors	1,143,974	1,153,291	1,252,319	1,252,319	1,129,089	784,044	685,460	808,690	907,274	981,212
Prepayments	58,016	48,266	61,466	51,716	41,966	55,166	45,416	35,666	48,866	39,116
Bank Account	(68,996)	(27,800)	89,828	281,561	370,895	432,752	139,845	(78,643)	(49,718)	22,437
	1,618,980	1,649,441	1,858,690	1,978,854	1,945,512	1,696,129	1,305,192	1,210,487	1,374,966	1,513,258
Current Liabilities										
Trade Creditors	446,295	469,118	505,980	483,527	469,909	275,222	118,075	56,613	176,070	273,704
Accruals	19,692	20,142	20,592	15,942	16,392	16,842	17,292	17,742	18,192	18,642
Corporation Tax	83,394	83,394	83,394	83,394	83,394	83,394	0	0	0	(30,000)
Proposed Dividend	120,000	120,000	120,000	120,000	120,000	120,000	0	0	0	0
Bank Overdraft	0	0	0	0	0	0	0	0	0	0
VAT	113,577	35,230	78,018	117,027	31,452	40,232	52,790	20,116	44,010	71,683
PAYE & NIC	36,706	36,706	36,706	36,706	36,706	36,706	36,706	36,706	36,706	36,706
	819,665	764,590	844,690	856,596	757,853	572,396	224,863	131,177	274,978	370,736
Net Current Assets	799,315	884,850	1,014,000	1,122,258	1,187,659	1,123,733	1,080,329	1,079,310	1,099,988	1,142,523
Assets Employed	1,004,909	1,087,844	1,214,394	1,320,052	1,382,853	1,316,327	1,270,323	1,266,704	1,284,782	1,324,717
Shareholders Funds										
Share Capital	20,000	20,000	20,000	20,000	20,000	20,000	20,000	20,000	20,000	20,000
Reserves	699,618	699,618	699,618	699,618	699,618	699,618	699,618	699,618	699,618	699,618
Profit & Loss A/c	285,292	368,227	494,776	600,434	663,235	596,710	550,705	547,086	565,165	605,099
	1,004,910	1,087,844	1,214,394	1,320,052	1,382,853	1,316,327	1,270,323	1,266,704	1,284,782	1,324,717

Corporation Tax	133,122
Dividend	200,000
	991,595

Good Business Limited

Monthly Balance Sheet Forecasts for the Year Ending 30th April 2000

	May £	June £	July £	August £	Sept £	October £	Nov £	December £	Jan £	Feb £	March £	April £
Fixed Assets												
Plant & Equipment	267,796	267,796	267,796	267,796	267,796	267,796	267,796	267,796	492,796	492,796	492,796	492,796
Fixtures, Fittings etc	11,294	11,294	11,294	11,294	11,294	11,294	11,294	11,294	11,294	11,294	11,294	11,294
Motor Vehicles	59,770	59,770	59,770	59,770	59,770	59,770	59,770	59,770	59,770	59,770	59,770	59,770
	338,860	338,860	338,860	338,860	338,860	338,860	338,860	338,860	563,860	563,860	563,860	563,860
Accumulated Depreciation	159,726	162,786	165,846	168,906	171,966	175,026	178,086	181,146	186,206	191,266	196,326	201,386
	179,134	176,074	173,014	169,954	166,894	163,834	160,774	157,714	377,654	372,594	367,534	362,474
Current Assets												
Stocks & WIP	469,519	470,679	492,345	481,512	459,846	394,848	405,681	427,347	438,180	449,013	473,676	475,718
Trade Debtors	1,126,076	1,195,627	1,195,627	1,198,888	1,306,679	1,306,679	1,175,455	808,026	703,047	834,271	939,251	1,017,985
Prepayments	54,613	69,812	58,913	48,014	63,213	52,314	41,415	56,614	45,715	34,816	50,015	39,116
Bank Account	20,888	152,637	352,121	395,147	531,870	746,708	851,845	963,076	374,985	172,093	155,402	228,999
	1,671,097	1,888,754	2,099,005	2,123,562	2,361,608	2,500,549	2,474,396	2,255,062	1,561,926	1,490,193	1,618,342	1,761,818
Current Liabilities												
Trade Creditors	358,041	423,255	483,721	475,806	484,020	435,421	431,442	319,794	226,939	193,334	277,247	338,540
Accruals	19,112	19,582	20,052	20,522	20,992	16,062	16,532	17,002	17,472	17,942	18,412	18,882
Corporation Tax	103,122	103,122	103,122	103,122	103,122	103,122	103,122	103,122	0	0	0	0
Proposed Dividend	200,000	200,000	200,000	200,000	200,000	200,000	200,000	200,000	0	0	0	0
Bank Overdraft	0	0	0	0	0	0	0	0	0	0	0	0
VAT	39,998	81,004	121,507	41,103	93,429	140,144	35,492	37,314	44,749	18,657	42,926	72,806
PAYE & NIC	36,706	36,706	36,706	36,706	36,706	36,706	36,706	36,706	36,706	36,706	36,706	36,706
	756,978	863,669	965,107	877,259	938,269	931,455	823,293	713,938	325,865	266,639	375,291	466,934
Net Current Assets	914,118	1,025,086	1,133,898	1,246,303	1,423,338	1,569,094	1,651,103	1,541,124	1,236,061	1,223,554	1,243,052	1,294,884
Assets Employed	1,093,252	1,201,160	1,306,912	1,416,257	1,590,232	1,732,928	1,811,877	1,698,838	1,613,715	1,596,148	1,610,586	1,657,358
Shareholders Funds												
Share Capital	20,000	20,000	20,000	20,000	20,000	20,000	20,000	20,000	20,000	20,000	20,000	20,000
Reserves	971,595	971,595	971,595	971,595	971,595	971,595	971,595	971,595	971,595	971,595	971,595	971,595
Profit & Loss A/c	101,658	209,565	315,317	424,662	598,637	741,333	820,282	707,243	622,120	604,553	618,991	665,763
	1,093,253	1,201,160	1,306,912	1,416,257	1,590,232	1,732,928	1,811,877	1,698,838	1,613,715	1,596,148	1,610,586	1,657,358

Corporation Tax	96,468
Dividend	250,000
	1,310,890

Good Business Limited

Monthly Balance Sheet Forecasts for the Year Ending 30th April 2001

	May £	June £	July £	August £	Sept £	October £	Nov £	December £	Jan £	Feb £	March £	April £
Fixed Assets												
Plant & Equipment	492,796	267,796	267,796	267,796	267,796	267,796	267,796	267,796	492,796	492,796	492,796	492,796
Fixtures, Fittings etc	11,294	11,294	11,294	11,294	11,294	11,294	11,294	11,294	11,294	11,294	11,294	11,294
Motor Vehicles	77,770	59,770	59,770	59,770	59,770	59,770	59,770	59,770	59,770	59,770	59,770	59,770
	581,860	338,860	338,860	338,860	338,860	338,860	338,860	338,860	563,860	563,860	563,860	563,860
Accumulated Depreciation	207,206	162,786	165,846	168,906	171,966	175,026	178,086	181,146	186,206	191,266	196,326	201,386
	374,654	176,074	173,014	169,954	166,894	163,834	160,774	157,714	377,654	372,594	367,534	362,474
Current Assets												
Stocks & WIP	474,697	470,679	492,345	481,512	459,846	394,848	405,681	427,347	438,180	449,013	473,676	475,718
Trade Debtors	1,169,349	1,195,627	1,195,627	1,198,888	1,306,679	1,306,679	1,175,455	808,026	703,047	834,271	939,251	1,017,985
Prepayments	54,499	72,697	60,101	47,504	65,702	53,106	40,509	58,707	46,111	33,514	51,712	39,116
Bank Account	199,157	331,783	548,743	599,002	745,894	978,786	1,094,852	1,215,073	811,288	597,674	577,520	656,301
	1,897,702	2,070,786	2,296,816	2,326,906	2,578,122	2,733,419	2,716,497	2,509,154	1,998,625	1,914,472	2,042,159	2,189,121
Current Liabilities												
Trade Creditors	407,334	466,355	530,658	522,373	531,038	480,122	475,927	358,673	261,167	225,868	197,220	259,427
Accruals	19,382	19,882	20,382	20,882	21,382	16,242	16,742	17,242	17,742	18,242	18,742	19,242
Corporation Tax	96,468	96,468	96,468	96,468	96,468	96,468	96,468	96,468	0	0	0	0
Proposed Dividend	250,000	250,000	250,000	250,000	250,000	250,000	250,000	250,000	0	0	0	0
Bank Overdraft	0	0	0	0	0	0	0	0	0	0	0	0
VAT	42,529	86,131	129,197	43,708	99,345	149,018	37,743	39,696	47,614	19,848	45,661	77,439
PAYE & NIC	36,706	36,706	36,706	36,706	36,706	36,706	36,706	36,706	36,706	36,706	36,706	36,706
	852,419	955,543	1,063,411	970,137	1,034,939	1,028,555	913,585	798,785	363,229	300,664	298,328	392,814
Net Current Assets	1,045,283	1,166,766	1,285,976	1,409,039	1,600,810	1,759,347	1,850,137	1,736,856	1,656,183	1,642,900	1,663,628	1,718,730
Assets Employed	1,419,937	1,342,840	1,458,990	1,578,993	1,767,704	1,923,181	2,010,911	1,894,570	2,033,837	2,015,494	2,031,162	2,081,204
Shareholders Funds												
Share Capital	20,000	20,000	20,000	20,000	20,000	20,000	20,000	20,000	20,000	20,000	20,000	20,000
Reserves	1,290,890	1,290,890	1,290,890	1,290,890	1,290,890	1,290,890	1,290,890	1,290,890	1,290,890	1,290,890	1,290,890	1,290,890
Profit & Loss A/c	109,047	224,710	338,101	455,344	641,296	794,013	878,984	759,883	673,390	654,288	669,196	718,479
	1,419,938	1,535,600	1,648,991	1,766,235	1,952,186	2,104,903	2,189,874	2,070,773	1,984,281	1,965,178	1,980,087	2,029,369

Corporation Tax	108,065
Dividend	300,000
	1,621,303

Good Business Limited

Cashflow Forecast for the Year Ending 30th April 1999

Actual 3 months to

	July	August	Sept	October	Nov	December	Jan	Feb	March	April	Total
	£	£	£	£	£	£	£	£	£	£	£
Receipts											
Debtors (45 days)	1,033,734	411,578	419,130	461,458	482,434	419,508	251,705	146,828	209,754	272,680	4,108,808
Vat @ 17.5%	180,903	72,026	73,348	80,755	84,426	73,414	44,048	25,695	36,707	47,719	719,041
	1,214,637	483,604	492,478	542,214	566,860	492,922	295,753	172,523	246,461	320,399	4,827,849
Payments											
Stock & Vatable Expenses (60 days)	615,144	190,000	210,000	205,048	218,192	258,909	238,551	197,833	75,681	96,040	2,305,398
Non Vat Expenses (Current)	11,287	3,705	3,705	3,705	3,705	3,705	3,705	3,705	3,705	3,705	44,632
Other Expenses											
Insurance	25,139	0	0	0	0	0	0	0	0	0	25,139
Rent & Rates	30,567	0	22,950	0	0	22,950	0	0	22,950	0	99,417
Audit & Accountancy	0	0	0	5,100	0	0	0	0	0	0	5,100
Wages +PAYE (Current)	306,126	101,774	101,774	101,774	101,774	101,774	101,774	101,774	101,774	101,774	1,222,092
Capital Expenditure:											
Plant & Equipment	0	0	0	0	0	0	0	0	0	0	0
Motor Vehicles	0	0	0	0	0	0	0	0	0	0	0
Corporation Tax/ACT	0	0	0	0	0	0	83,394	0	0	30,000	113,394
Dividends	0	0	0	0	0	0	120,000	0	0	0	120,000
Input Vat	107,650	33,250	36,750	35,883	38,184	45,309	41,746	34,621	13,244	16,807	403,445
Vat Quarterly Returns	73,129	113,577	0	0	117,027	0	0	52,790	0	0	356,523
	1,169,042	442,306	375,179	351,510	478,881	432,648	589,171	390,723	217,354	248,326	4,695,140
Bank Account											
Opening Balance	(113,840)	(68,996)	(27,800)	89,828	281,561	370,895	432,754	139,849	(78,640)	(49,715)	(113,840)
Movement in Month	45,595	41,298	117,299	190,703	87,979	60,274	(293,418)	(218,201)	29,106	72,073	132,709
	(68,245)	(27,698)	89,499	280,531	369,540	431,169	139,336	(78,352)	(49,534)	22,358	18,869
Interest @ 4.5%	(751)	(102)	328	1,030	1,356	1,582	511	(288)	(182)	82	3,566
Closing Balance	(68,996)	(27,800)	89,827	281,561	370,896	432,751	139,847	(78,640)	(49,716)	22,440	22,435

Good Business Limited

Cashflow Forecast for the Year Ending 30th April 2000

	May	June	July	August	Sept	October	Nov	December	Jan	Feb	March	April	Total
	£	£	£	£	£	£	£	£	£	£	£	£	£
Receipts													
Debtors (45 days)	314,631	386,763	441,937	443,946	444,329	491,394	513,730	446,722	268,033	156,353	223,361	290,369	4,421,566
Vat @ 17.5%	55,060	67,683	77,339	77,690	77,758	85,994	89,903	78,176	46,906	27,362	39,088	50,815	773,774
	369,691	454,446	519,276	521,636	522,087	577,388	603,633	524,898	314,939	183,714	262,449	341,184	5,195,340
Payments													
Vatable Expenses (60 days)	136,757	157,116	177,475	209,362	211,630	210,496	211,846	237,059	224,453	199,240	123,601	136,207	2,235,241
Non Vat Expenses (Current)	3,903	3,903	3,903	3,903	3,903	3,903	3,903	3,903	3,903	3,903	3,903	3,903	46,841
Other Expenses													
Insurance	26,396	0	0	0	0	0	0	0	0	0	0	0	26,396
Rent & Rates	0	26,097	0	0	26,097	0	0	26,097	0	0	26,097	0	104,388
Audit & Accountancy	0	0	0	0	0	5,400	0	0	0	0	0	0	5,400
Wages +PAYE (Current)	108,644	108,644	108,644	108,644	108,644	108,644	108,644	108,644	108,644	104,477	104,477	104,477	1,291,225
Capital Expenditure:													
Plant & Equipment	0	0	0	0	0	0	0	0	225,000	0	0	0	225,000
Motor Vehicles	0	0	0	0	0	0	0	0	0	0	0	0	0
Corporation Tax	0	0	0	0	0	0	0	0	103,122	0	0	0	103,122
Dividends	0	0	0	0	0	0	0	0	200,000	0	0	0	200,000
Input Vat	23,933	27,495	31,058	36,638	37,035	36,837	37,073	41,485	39,279	34,867	21,630	23,836	391,167
Vat Quarterly Returns	71,683	0	0	121,507	0	0	140,144	0	0	44,749	0	0	378,083
	371,316	323,255	321,080	480,054	387,309	365,280	501,611	417,189	904,401	387,236	279,708	268,424	5,006,862
Bank Account													
Opening Balance	22,437	20,888	152,637	352,121	395,147	531,870	746,708	851,845	963,076	374,985	172,093	155,402	22,437
Movement in Month	(1,625)	131,191	198,196	41,582	134,778	212,108	102,022	107,709	(589,462)	(203,521)	(17,259)	72,760	188,477
	20,812	152,079	350,833	393,702	529,925	743,978	848,730	959,554	373,613	171,463	154,833	228,161	210,914
Interest @ 4.5%	76	558	1,288	1,445	1,945	2,730	3,115	3,522	1,371	629	568	837	18,085
Closing Balance	20,888	152,637	352,121	395,147	531,870	746,708	851,845	963,076	374,985	172,093	155,402	228,999	228,999

Good Business Limited

Cashflow Forecast for the Year Ending 30th April 2000

	May	June	July	August	Sept	October	Nov	December	Jan	Feb	March	April	Total
	£	£	£	£	£	£	£	£	£	£	£	£	£
Receipts													
Debtors (45 days)	335,041	410,619	468,117	470,245	470,664	520,531	544,192	473,210	283,926	165,624	236,605	307,587	4,686,360
Vat @ 17.5%	58,632	71,858	81,920	82,293	82,366	91,093	95,234	82,812	49,687	28,984	41,406	53,828	820,113
	393,673	482,478	550,037	552,538	553,030	611,624	639,425	556,022	333,613	194,608	278,011	361,414	5,506,473
Payments													
Vatable Expenses (60 days)	161,420	174,027	186,633	220,837	223,218	222,027	223,452	249,923	236,688	210,216	130,802	144,038	2,383,281
Non Vat Expenses (Current)	4,109	4,109	4,109	4,109	4,109	4,109	4,109	4,109	4,109	4,109	4,109	4,109	49,312
Other Expenses													
Insurance	27,980	0	0	0	0	0	0	0	0	0	0	0	27,980
Rent & Rates	0	30,794	0	0	30,794	0	0	30,794	0	0	30,794	0	123,178
Audit & Accountancy	0	0	0	0	0	5,640	0	0	0	0	0	0	5,640
Wages +PAYE (Current)	111,680	111,680	111,680	111,680	111,680	111,680	111,680	111,680	111,680	111,680	111,680	111,680	1,340,158
Capital Expenditure:													
Plant & Equipment	0	0	0	0	0	0	0	0	0	0	0	0	0
Motor Vehicles	18,000	0	0	0	0	0	0	0	0	0	0	0	18,000
Corporation Tax	0	0	0	0	0	0	0	0	96,468	0	0	0	96,468
Dividends	0	0	0	0	0	0	0	0	250,000	0	0	0	250,000
Input Vat	28,249	30,455	32,661	38,646	39,063	38,855	39,104	43,737	41,420	36,788	22,890	25,207	417,074
Vat Quarterly Returns	72,806	0	0	129,197	0	0	149,018	0	0	47,614	0	0	398,635
	424,244	351,065	335,083	504,470	408,864	382,311	527,363	440,243	740,365	410,407	300,276	285,034	5,109,726
Bank Account													
Opening Balance	228,999	199,157	331,783	548,743	599,002	745,894	978,786	1,094,852	1,215,073	811,288	597,674	577,520	228,999
Movement in Month	(30,570)	131,413	214,954	48,068	144,165	229,313	112,062	115,778	(406,752)	(215,800)	(22,265)	76,381	396,748
	198,428	330,569	546,737	596,811	743,167	975,207	1,090,848	1,210,630	808,321	595,488	575,409	653,901	625,746
Interest @ 4.5%	728	1,213	2,007	2,190	2,727	3,579	4,003	4,443	2,967	2,185	2,112	2,400	30,555
Closing Balance	199,157	331,783	548,743	599,002	745,894	978,786	1,094,852	1,215,073	811,288	597,674	577,520	656,301	656,301

Sample Financial Projections

Good Business Limited

Assumptions

1 Inflation has been ignored.
2 Interest rates will remain constant.
3 There will be no change in the nature or seasonality of the trade.
4 The $:£ exchange rate will average 1.65.
5 Customers will pay on average 45 days after invoicing.
6 Suppliers will be paid on average 60 days from date of supply.
7 VAT, PAYE and NIC will be paid on time.
8 Wages and salaries will be paid in the month in which they are incurred.
9 Corporation tax and dividends are ignored in the detailed P & L Accounts.
10 Deferred tax is ignored.
11 New production staff and/or overtime will be available to meet requirements.
12 A new Sales person will commence in May 1999.
13 A new automated finishing line will be installed in January 2000 producing salary savings of £50k pa.
14 Each year approximately 7.5% of customers will convert to our own product.
15 Suppliers of factored goods will hold prices to maintain market share.

Appendix IV

Sample Confidentiality Agreement

STRICTLY PRIVATE & CONFIDENTIAL

To: Potential Purchasers and Investors

CONFIDENTIALITY UNDERTAKING AND INDEMNITY

Gentlemen

The vendor, whose name will be disclosed, is going to provide you on a non-exclusive basis with information (verbal and written) to enable you, as a Potential Purchaser or Investor ("PPI"), to determine whether or not to pursue enquiries with a view to purchasing either shares in the company, the business or making loans or any other form of investment. The information may not be used for any other purpose.

The PPI accepts that the information does not and shall not be deemed to constitute any representation or warranty by anyone as to its accuracy, completeness or reasonableness. MacIntyre Corporate Finance Ltd ("MCF") shall have no liability whatsoever to the PPI or anyone else resulting from the use of the information.

By signing this letter, the PPI acknowledges that the information provided is strictly confidential and that the vendor may suffer material commercial loss if such confidentiality is breached. The PPI agrees not to use any of such information for the PPI's own benefit (except in evaluating the investment potential of this particular sale) or for the benefit of others.

Except for information already in the public domain (other than as a result of a breach of this agreement), the PPI also agrees to keep permanently confidential the information provided and may not copy, reproduce or distribute to others any of the information without the prior written consent of the vendor. The PPI will, upon request, immediately return all information received in connection therewith, without retaining copies thereof following which the PPI will use its best efforts to prevent the disclosure of any information. The PPI also agrees not to make any announcements or disclose their prospective interest in the vendor or its business without the written consent of the vendor except where required by law or under the rules of a recognised Stock Exchange in which case the PPI agrees to consult with the vendor prior to such announcement.

The PPI agrees not to contact directly or indirectly the vendor, its employees or customers except with the explicit consent of MCF.

The PPI hereby agree to indemnify and hold the vendor harmless from any loss which the vendor may incur or be subject to by reason of the breach of any provision of this letter by the PPI.

The PPI acknowledges that the vendors are acting in reliance upon the undertakings and indemnity set out above in the provision of information to the PPI.

You shall ensure that your employees, officers, agents, or

professional advisors and all or any other third party to whom you make disclosure are aware of the need for secrecy and confidentiality, and will extract a similar written undertaking from them in the vendor's favour. You shall only disclose such matters as are necessary for evaluation and negotiation.

On acceptance of the terms of this document, you shall sign and return it to MCF.

Agreed to accepted
this day of   19

BY:

On behalf of:

(as Potential Purchaser or Investor)

Appendix V

Sample Sale and Purchase Agreement* relating to the sale of the whole of the issued share capital of Target Limited

(* Supplied courtesy of Edwin Coe, Solicitors, 2 Stone Buildings, Lincoln's Inn, London WC2A 3TH)

INDEX TO CLAUSES

117

– The Company's Business
– Consequences of Sale of the Shares

Schedule 5	The properties
Schedule 6	Pensions
Schedule 7	Intellectual property
Schedule 8	Agreed forms
Schedule 9	Agreed accounting principles

SHARE PURCHASE AGREEMENT

Date:

PARTIES:

(1)　The Disposing Company Ltd (Registered No. [ ]) whose registered office is at [ ] ("the Vendors"); and

(2)　The Purchasing Company Plc (Registered No. [ ]) whose registered office is at [ ] ("the Purchaser").

RECITALS:

A.　The Company is a private company limited by shares. Details of the Company are set out in Schedule 1.

B.　The Vendors have agreed to sell and the Purchaser has agreed to buy the Shares on the terms and subject to the conditions of this Agreement.

AGREEMENT:

1　Definitions and Interpretation

1.1　The Recitals and Schedules form part of this Agreement and shall have the same force and effect as if set out in the body of this Agreement. Any reference to this Agreement shall include the Recitals and Schedules.

1.2　In this Agreement, the following words and expressions shall have the following meanings:-

"THE ACCOUNTS" the audited accounts of the Company and each of the Subsidiaries for the accounting reference period which ended on the Accounts Date (comprising in each case a balance sheet and profit and loss account, notes and directors' and auditors' reports), a copy of each of which is annexed to the Disclosure Letter;

"THE ACCOUNTS DATE" [ ];

"THE AGREED FORM" the form agreed between and signed by or on behalf of the Vendors and the Purchaser, the Agreed Form documents referred to in this Agreement being listed in Schedule 8;

"AGREED ACCOUNTING PRINCIPLES" the accounting principles and policies to be applied in the preparation of the Completion Accounts as set out in Schedule 9;

"BASE RATE" the base rate of [ ] Bank plc for the time being and from time to time;

"CAA 1990" Capital Allowances Act 1990;

"CERTIFICATE" the certificate of the value of the Net Assets prepared by the Vendors' Auditors and agreed between the Parties pursuant to clauses 4.2 to 4.5;

"CGA 1992" Taxation of Chargeable Gains Act 1992;

"THE COMPANY" Target Limited details of which are set out in Schedule 1;

"THE COMPANIES ACTS" the Companies Act 1985, the Criminal Justice Act 1993 (insofar as it relates to insider dealing), the Companies Consolidation (Consequential Provisions) Act 1985 and the Companies Act 1989;

"COMPLETION" completion of the sale and purchase of the Shares in accordance with this Agreement;

"COMPLETION ACCOUNTS" the audited consolidated balance sheet of the Company and the Subsidiaries as at the date of Completion and the audited consolidated profit and loss account of the Company and the Subsidiaries in respect of the period from the Accounts Date to the date of Completion;

"THE COMPLETION DATE" [ ];

"THE CONSIDERATION" the sum referred to in Clause 4.1;

"THE DISCLOSURE LETTER" the letter dated the date of this Agreement from the Vendors to the Purchaser making certain disclosures against the Warranties;

"THE ENVIRONMENTAL DEED" The environmental deed to be entered into between the Vendors and the Purchaser marked "I";

"ENVIRONMENTAL LAWS" all European Community legislation, regulations, directives, decisions and judgments all statutes and subordinate legislation, all regulations and orders, all common law and other national, international and local laws and bye-laws, all judgements, orders, instructions or awards of any court or competent authority and all codes of practice and guidance notes and circulars which:-

(a)   have as a purpose or effect the protection or enhancement of the environment and relate to the presence, manufacturing, processing, treatment, keeping, handling, use, possession, supply, receiving, sale, purchase, import, export or transportation of Hazardous Materials or any event, activity, condition or phenomenon which alone or in combination with others is capable of causing harm or damage to property or to man or any other organism supported by the environment;

(b)   relate to the release, spillage, deposit, escape, discharge, leak or emission of Hazardous Materials;

(c)   relate to the control of Waste;

(d)   relate to noise, vibration, radiation or common law or statutory nuisance or any other interference with the enjoyment or use of land;

(e)   relate to the use of land or the erection, occupation or use of buildings or other natural or man-made structures above or below ground; or

(f)   relate to human health and safety;

"THE EXECUTIVES" [ ];

"GROUP COMPANY" the Company and the Subsidiaries;

"HAZARDOUS MATERIAL" any substance or organism which alone or in combination with others is capable of causing harm or damage to property or to man or any other organism supported by the environment or to the environment or public health or welfare;

"ICTA" Income and Corporation Taxes Act 1988;

"INDEPENDENT ACCOUNTANT" the accountant nominated or appointed pursuant to Clause 4.7;

"MANAGEMENT ACCOUNTS" the unaudited [consolidated] [balance sheet and profit and loss account of the Company [and the Subsidiaries] as at [ ] 1995 in the Agreed Form;

"NET ASSETS" the aggregate of the assets of the Group Companies less the aggregate of their liabilities as shown in the balance sheet forming part of the Completion Accounts and as certified in the Certificate;

"THE PARTIES" the parties to this Agreement;

"THE PROPERTIES" the freehold and leasehold properties of the Company and the Subsidiaries, details of which are given in Schedule 5;

"THE PURCHASER'S AUDITORS" [ ];

"THE PURCHASER'S SOLICITORS" [ ];

"THE RESTRICTED TERRITORIES" all countries and territories worldwide;

"THE SHARES" the shares referred to in paragraph 8 of Schedule 1 comprising the entire issued share capital of the Company;

"THE SUBSIDIARIES" the subsidiaries and associated companies of the Company as at the Completion Date details of which are set out in Schedule 2;

["THE SERVICE AGREEMENTS" the service agreements proposed to be entered into between the Company and the Executives being in the Agreed Form marked "Al" to "A[ ]"];

"TAXATION" liability arising under any of the Taxation Statutes;

"TAXATION STATUTES" statutes (and all regulations and arrangements whatsoever made thereunder) enacted (or issued coming into force or entered into) whether before or after the date of this Agreement providing for or imposing or relating to all forms of taxation, duties, levies and rates whatsoever including without limitation:-

(a) any charge, tax, duty or levy upon income, profits, chargeable gains or any other property or instruments in writing or supplies or other transactions;

(b) income tax, corporation tax, advance corporation tax, withholding tax, capital gains tax, inheritance tax, value added tax, stamp duty, stamp duty reserve tax, customs and other import duties, national insurance contributions, general rates, water rates or other local rates;

(c) any liability for sums equivalent to any such charge, tax, duty, levy or rates and/or for any penalty, fine or interest payable in connection therewith;

(d) any law or regulation whatsoever providing for or imposing or otherwise relating to any charge, tax, levy or rates (of a like or similar nature) chargeable outside the United Kingdom and/or for any penalty, fine or interest payable in connection with them;

"TAX WARRANTIES" the Warranties in paragraph 5 of schedule 4 and any other Warranty so far as it relates to Taxation;

"THE TAX DEED" the tax deed to be entered into between the Vendors and the Purchaser in the Agreed Form marked "B";

"VATA 1994" Value Added Tax Act 1994;

"THE VENDORS' AUDITORS" [ ];

"THE VENDORS' SOLICITORS" [ ];

"THE WARRANTIES" the representations, warranties and undertakings set out in Schedule 4;

"WASTE" includes any substance which constitutes a scrap material or an effluent or other unwanted surplus substance arising from the application of any process and any substance or article which is or is intended or required to be disposed of.

1.3 In this Agreement (unless the context requires otherwise) :-

1.3.1 words and expressions which are defined in the Companies Acts shall have the same meanings as are ascribed to them in the Companies Acts;

1.3.2 any question as to whether a person is connected with any other person shall be determined in accordance with the provisions of Section 839 ICTA;

1.3.3 any reference to any statute or statutory provision shall be construed as including a reference to any modification, consolidation, re-enactment or extension of such statute or statutory provision for the time being in force, to any subordinate legislation made under the same and to any former statute or statutory provision which it consolidated or re-enacted;

1.3.4 any reference to a SSAP or a FRS respectively is to a Statement of Standard Accounting Practice published by the Consultative Committee of Accounting Bodies of England and Wales as amended from time to time or a Financial Reporting Standard published by the Accounting Standards Board as amended from time to time;

1.3.5 any gender includes a reference to all other genders;

1.3.6 the singular includes a reference to the plural and vice versa;

1.3.7 any reference to a Recital, Clause or Schedule is to a Recital, Clause or Schedule (as the case may be) of or to this Agreement;

1.3.8 "directly or indirectly" shall (without limiting the expression) mean either alone or jointly with any other person, firm or body corporate and whether on his own account or in partnership with another or others or as the holder of any interest in or as officer, employee or agent of or consultant to any other person, firm or body corporate; and

1.3.9 any reference to any English legal term for any action, remedy, method of judicial proceeding, legal document, legal status, court, official or any legal concept or thing shall, in respect of any jurisdiction other than England, be deemed to include what most nearly approximates in that jurisdiction to the English legal term.

1.4 The headings contained in this Agreement are for the purposes of convenience only and do not form part of and shall not affect the construction of this Agreement or any part of it.

2   Conditions

2.1 This Agreement shall be conditional in all respects upon:-

2.1.1 the Secretary of State for Trade and Industry confirming in terms satisfactory to the Purchaser that it is not his intention to refer any of the transactions contemplated by this Agreement or matters arising therefrom to the Monopolies and Mergers Commission in exercise of his powers under the Fair Trading Act 1973; and

2.1.2 the Purchaser having completed to its satisfaction an environmental audit relating to the business of the Company and the Subsidiaries.

2.2 If the conditions set out in Clause 2.1 shall not have been satisfied by the opening of business hours on the Completion Date, this Agreement (except for the provisions of this Clause and of Clauses 10 and 11.3) shall, unless waived by the Purchaser by notice in writing to the Vendors, be null and void and of no further effect and the Parties shall be released and discharged from their respective obligations under this Agreement.

3   Sale and Purchase

3.1   The Vendors shall sell with full title guarantee free from all liens, charges and encumbrances and the Purchaser relying on the representations, undertakings and indemnities by the Vendors in this Agreement shall purchase the Shares with effect from and including the Completion Date to the intent that as from that date all rights and advantages accruing to the Shares, including any dividends or distributions declared or paid on the Shares after that date, shall belong to the Purchaser.

3.2   The Purchaser shall not be obliged to complete the purchase of any of the Shares unless the sale of all of the Shares is completed simultaneously.

4   Consideration and Adjustment to Consideration

4.1   Subject to adjustment in accordance with the provisions of this Agreement, the consideration for the Shares shall be the sum of £[ ] payable in cash at completion to [ ].

4.2   The Parties shall jointly procure as soon as practicable and in any event within [60] days of the date of Completion that a draft of the Completion Accounts and a draft certificate of the value of the Net Assets are prepared by the Vendors' Auditors on the basis of the Agreed Accounting Principles and submitted to the Purchaser's Auditors for their consideration.

4.3   The Parties shall respectively disclose all information necessary to prepare the draft Completion Accounts and the Purchaser's Auditors shall be given access to the Vendors' Auditors working papers in relation to the Completion Accounts and the Certificate.

4.4   The Parties shall use their respective reasonable endeavours to agree the draft Completion Accounts and the draft Certificate as soon as reasonably practicable. Failing agreement within 30 days of the receipt by the Purchaser's Auditors of the draft Completion Accounts and the draft Certificate, any dispute or difference relating thereto shall be referred for final determination to an Independent Accountant nominated jointly by the Vendors and the Purchaser or failing such nomination at the request of either party by the President for the time being of the Institute of Chartered Accountants in England and Wales. The Independent Accountant shall be instructed to render his decision within 30 days of his nomination or appointment and shall act as an expert and not as an arbitrator and (in the absence of manifest error) his decision (which shall be communicated in writing to the Vendors and the Purchaser) shall be final and binding on the Vendors and the Purchaser. The fees and costs of the Independent Accountant shall be borne and paid by the Vendors and the Purchaser in such proportions as the Independent Accountant shall consider appropriate.

4.5   The Parties shall procure that the draft Completion Accounts as so agreed or determined shall be audited and certified by the Vendors' Auditors who shall also be instructed to issue to the Parties the Certificate in the form of the draft as so agreed or determined. The Certificate shall be final and binding on the Parties.

4.6   The Vendors warrant to the Purchaser that the Net Assets shall be not less than £ [ ].

4.7   If the Net Assets shall amount to less than £[ ] the Consideration shall be reduced by the amount of the shortfall but so that the amount of such reduction shall be limited to the amount or value of the Consideration.

4.8   The Vendors shall pay the amount of any shortfall in the Net Assets calculated pursuant to Clause 4.7 to the Purchaser in cash within seven days after delivery of the Completion Accounts and the Certificate pursuant to Clause 4.5 and failing payment in full within seven days the balance outstanding from time to time shall bear interest from the Completion Date until actual payment at the Base Rate.

5 Completion

5.1   Completion shall take place on the Completion Date at [ ] or such other place as the Purchaser may require when:-

   5.1.1   the Vendors shall deliver to the Purchaser, or procure the delivery to the Purchaser of, the documents referred to in Schedule 3;

   5.1.2   the Vendors and the Purchaser shall jointly procure that there shall be held a Meeting of the Board of Directors of the Company and of each of the Subsidiaries at which there shall be duly passed resolutions set out and contained in board minutes of the Company and the Subsidiaries in the Agreed Form marked "Fl" to "F[ ]" respectively;

   5.1.3   the Purchaser shall deliver to the Vendors' Solicitors:-

      5.1.3.1 a bankers draft for £[ ] (or alternatively transfer the same by telegraphic transfer), being the purchase price for the Shares receipt of which shall constitute good discharge from both Vendors; and

      5.1.3.2 a counterpart of the Tax Deed and the Environmental Deed duly executed by the Purchaser.

5.2   The performance by the Vendors of their obligations under Clause 5.1 shall be a condition precedent to the performance by the Purchaser of its obligations under Clause 5.1 to the intent that, if the Vendors fail or shall be unable to perform any of such obligations, the Purchaser shall at its option (and without prejudice to any other remedies or rights which it may have against the Vendors in respect of such non-performance) stipulate a new date for completion or rescind this Agreement in which case it will cease to be liable to perform its obligations under Clause 5.1.

6   Period before Completion

6.1   The Vendors undertake to and covenant with the Purchaser that they will procure that between the date of this Agreement and Completion:-

6.1.1   no increase shall be made in the authorised, allotted or issued share capitals of the Company or any of the Subsidiaries;

6.1.2   no option, right of conversion, or right of pre-emption shall be offered or granted by the Company or any of the Subsidiaries over the whole or any part of their respective share capitals, whether issued or unissued; and

6.1.3   no dividends or other distributions shall be declared, made or paid by the Company or any of the Subsidiaries.

6.2   The Vendors further undertake to and covenant with the Purchaser that they will procure that between the date of this Agreement and Completion (save with the previous written consent of the Purchaser):-

6.2.1   the business of the Company and each of the Subsidiaries shall be carried on in the ordinary and usual course and so as to maintain the same as a going concern and with a view to profit;

6.2.2   the Company and each of the Subsidiaries shall take all reasonable steps to preserve and protect its business and assets and notify the Purchaser in writing promptly of any adverse change in such business or assets;

6.2.3   the Purchaser and its advisers are given promptly on request such facilities and information regarding the business, assets, liabilities, contracts and affairs of the Company and of the Subsidiaries as the Purchaser may require;

6.2.4   all existing insurance policies relating to the Company and the Subsidiaries and all guarantees and indemnities relating to the business of the Company and the Subsidiaries shall be maintained in full force and effect and shall not be allowed to lapse, expire or be forfeited or otherwise terminated;

6.2.5   neither the Company nor any of the Subsidiaries shall:-

6.2.5.1   alter or agree to alter or terminate or agree to terminate any agreement to which it is a party or enter or agree to enter into any unusual or abnormal contract or commitment or any contract or commitment with the Vendors or their affiliates or persons connected with the Vendors;

6.2.5.2   incur any material capital expenditure or any material capital commitment or dispose of or realise any material capital asset or any interest in any such asset and for the purpose of this clause the sum of £[ ] or more shall be classified as material;

6.2.5.3 create or agree to create any mortgage, charge, lien or encumbrance over all or any of its assets (other than liens arising in the ordinary course of business) or redeem or agree to redeem any existing security or give or agree to give any guarantee or indemnity;

6.2.5.4 alter or agree to alter the terms of any existing borrowing facilities or arrange any additional borrowing facilities;

6.2.5.5 increase or agree to increase the remuneration (including, without limitation, pension contributions, bonuses, commissions and benefits in kind) of any director or employee or provide or agree to provide any gratuitous payment or benefit to any such person or any of his dependants and no employee shall be engaged or dismissed or have his terms of employment altered;

6.2.5.6 create, incur, or assume any debt, liability or obligation, direct or indirect, whether accrued, absolute, contingent or otherwise, other than in the ordinary course of business consistent with past practice;

6.2.5.7 waive or release any rights of material value;

6.2.5.8 transfer, sell or otherwise convey any of its assets, other than the sale of inventory in the ordinary course of business consistent with past practice;

6.2.5.9 make any material alteration in the manner of keeping its books, accounts or records, or in the accounting practices therein reflected, except as required by law or generally accepted accounting principles;

6.2.5.10 accelerate or delay the manufacture, shipment or sale of inventory, the collection of accounts or notes receivable or the payment of accounts or notes payable or otherwise operate its business in a manner designed to affect artificially the computation of the Net Assets;

6.2.5.11 agree or otherwise commit to take any of the actions referred to in the subsections above.

6.3 The Vendors shall procure that, between the date of this Agreement and Completion, reasonable advance notice shall be given to the Purchaser of all Meetings of the Board of Directors (or of Committees of the Directors) of the Company and each of the Subsidiaries (together with an agenda of the business to be transacted at such Meetings and all supporting documentation) and that duly authorised representatives of the Purchaser (not being more than two in number at any one time) shall be permitted to attend and participate in such Meetings.

6.4 The Vendors shall, and shall procure that the officers and employees of and the professional advisers to the Company and each of the Subsidiaries shall, between the date of this Agreement and Completion on the request of the Purchaser supply the Purchaser and/or its professional advisers with such information concerning the Company and the Subsidiaries as the Purchaser or its professional advisers may reasonably require and give the Purchaser and its professional advisers access to any of the Properties.

6.5 The Purchaser shall be entitled by written notice to the Vendors to rescind this Agreement if there is any breach of any of the provisions of Clauses 6.1 to 6.4. The exercise of such right shall not extinguish any right to damages to which the Purchaser may be entitled in respect of any such breach. Failure to exercise such right shall not constitute a waiver of any other rights of the Purchaser arising out of any such breach.

7   Warranties and Indemnity

7.1 The Vendors represent, warrant and undertake to the Purchaser that:-

7.1.1 each of the Warranties is true and accurate in all respects and is not misleading at the date of this Agreement;

7.1.2 the contents of the Disclosure Letter and of all documents referred to in or accompanying it are true, accurate and complete in all respects and fully, clearly and accurately disclose every matter to which they relate;

7.1.3 there are fully and accurately disclosed in the Disclosure Letter all matters which are necessary to qualify the Warranties in order for the Warranties when so qualified to be fair, accurate and not misleading; and

7.1.4 each of the Warranties will be fulfilled down to and will remain true and accurate in all respects and not misleading at Completion as if they had been entered into afresh at Completion by reference to the facts and circumstances then existing.

7.2 The Warranties shall not in any respect be extinguished or affected by Completion.

7.3 The Vendors undertake to the Purchaser that if, between the date of this Agreement and Completion, any event (including for the avoidance of doubt any omission) occurs which results, or which may result, in any of the Warranties being unfulfilled, untrue or inaccurate at Completion then they will immediately and in any event before Completion give the Purchaser written notice of that event and its consequences.

7.4 If, before Completion, it is found that any of the Warranties has not been fulfilled or is untrue or inaccurate the Purchaser shall be entitled by notice in writing given to the other Parties before Completion to rescind this Agreement but failure to exercise this right shall not constitute a waiver of any other rights of the Purchaser or its successors in title arising out of any of the Warranties being unfulfilled, untrue or inaccurate. Rescission of this Agreement under this Clause shall not extinguish any right to damages to which the Purchaser or its successors in title may be entitled in respect of the breach of this Agreement.

7.5 If, between the date of this Agreement and Completion, any event shall occur (other than an event constituting or giving rise to a breach of any of the Warranties) which affects or is likely to affect adversely to a material degree the financial position or business prospects of the Company and the Subsidiaries (not being an event affecting or likely to affect generally all companies carrying on similar businesses in the United Kingdom) the Purchaser shall be entitled by notice in writing to the other Parties to rescind this Agreement (but the occurrence of such an event shall not give rise to any right to damages or compensation).

7.6 The Vendors acknowledges that the Purchaser has entered into this Agreement in reliance on representations in the terms of the Warranties with the intention of inducing the Purchaser to enter into this Agreement and that accordingly the Purchaser has been induced by those representations to enter into this Agreement.

7.7 The Vendors undertake to the Purchaser that, in the event of any claim being made against it for breach of the Warranties or under the Tax Covenant, it will not make any claim against the Company or any of the Subsidiaries or against any director, officer or employee of the Company or any of the Subsidiaries on which or on whom it may have relied before agreeing to any terms of this Agreement or of the Tax Deed or authorising any statement in the Disclosure Letter.

7.8 The Warranties:-

7.8.1 are qualified by reference to those matters fully, fairly and clearly disclosed in the Disclosure Letter and not otherwise. In particular, but without limitation, the rights and remedies of the Purchaser in respect of the Warranties shall not be affected by any investigation made by or on behalf of the Purchaser into the affairs of the Company and the Subsidiaries;

7.8.2 are separate and independent and, unless expressly provided to the contrary, are not limited or restricted by reference to or inference from the terms of any other provision of this Agreement or any other Warranty;

7.8.3 where qualified by the knowledge, information, belief or awareness of the Vendors, are deemed to include a statement that such knowledge, information, belief or awareness has been acquired after due and careful enquiries by the Vendors in respect of the relevant subject matter of such Warranties; and

7.8.4 apply to each of the Subsidiaries as well as to the Company as if the word "Company" was defined to mean each of the Subsidiaries and the Company.

7.9 The liability of the Vendors under the Warranties (other than the Tax Warranties) shall cease on the third anniversary of the Completion Date and under the Tax Deed and the Tax Warranties on the seventh anniversary of the Completion Date except as regards any alleged specific breach of this Agreement and any of the Warranties or any specific claim under the Tax Deed in respect of which notice in writing has been served on the Vendors prior to that date provided that no such limitations shall apply to the Warranties referred to in paragraphs 6.7.1 to 6.7.17 of Schedule 4 and provided further that no such limitations shall apply in relation to the Warranties and the Tax Deed generally in the event of fraud and/or dishonesty.

7.10 The Vendors shall not be liable for any claims arising from breach of any of the Warranties or any claim for indemnity pursuant to the Tax Deed unless their aggregate liability (or what would be such liability apart from this clause) exceeds £50,000 and in that event the Vendors shall be liable for the amount of all such claims.

7.11 The Vendors shall indemnify and hereby undertake to keep indemnified the Purchaser or at the option of the Purchaser, the Companies against all liabilities, costs, damages and expenses (including legal expenses) which may be incurred or suffered directly or indirectly by the Purchaser or any of the Group Companies arising from, or relating to:-

7.11.1 any breach or any violation of any of the Warranties; or

7.11.2 any failure by the Vendors to perform or otherwise fulfil or comply with any provision of the Agreement; or

7.11.3 the sale by any of the Group Companies prior to the Completion Date of any business, assets, shares or stock.

8 Restrictions on the Vendors

8.1 The Vendors covenant with the Purchaser with the intention of assuring to the Purchaser the full benefit and value of the goodwill and connections of the Company and the Subsidiaries and as a constituent part of the agreement for the sale of the Shares that save with the previous written consent of the Purchaser:-

8.1.1 they will not in the Restricted Territories for the period of five years following the Completion Date directly or indirectly deal with or engage in business with or be in any way interested in or connected with any concern, undertaking, firm or body corporate which engages in or carries on within any part of the Restricted Territories any business which competes with any business of a kind carried on by the Company or any of the Subsidiaries at the Completion Date and in particular (but without limitation) the business of [ ];

8.1.2 they will not in the Restricted Territories for the period of five years following the Completion Date directly or indirectly:-

8.1.1.1 interfere with or, in competition with the Company or any of the Subsidiaries, offer or agree to provide goods or services of any description to, or solicit or endeavour to entice away from the Company or any of the Subsidiaries the custom of any person, firm or body corporate which, at any time during the period of two years ending on the Completion Date, has been a customer or client of, or in the habit of dealing with, the Company or any of the Subsidiaries or which, at any time during that period, was to his knowledge negotiating with the Company or any of the Subsidiaries in relation to the provision of goods or services by the Company or any of the Subsidiaries;

8.1.1.2 interfere or seek to interfere with contractual or other trade relations between the Company or any of the Subsidiaries and any of its or their respective suppliers in existence or under negotiation at any time during the period of two years ending on the Completion Date;

8.1.1.3 solicit the services of or endeavour to entice away from the Company or any of the Subsidiaries any director, employee or consultant of the Company or any of the Subsidiaries in an executive technical or sales capacity (whether or not such person would commit any breach of his contract of employment or engagement by reason of leaving the service of such company) or knowingly employ, assist in or procure the employment by any other person, firm or body corporate of any such person;

8.1.3 they will not at any time following the Completion Date disclose to any person, firm or body corporate or otherwise make use or permit the use of any trade secrets or confidential knowledge or information concerning the business, finance or affairs of the Company or any of the Subsidiaries or any of their respective customers, clients or suppliers and will use their best endeavours to prevent the publication or disclosure of any such secrets, knowledge or information by any third party;

8.1.4 they will not at any time following the Completion Date unless specifically authorised by the Purchaser use for any purpose any trade or business name, trade mark or service mark used by the Company or any of the Subsidiaries preceding the Completion Date including in particular (but without limitation) the names [" ", " ", " " [others]] (whether alone or in conjunction with other names) or any name similar to those names or likely to be confused with them.

8.2 The Vendors covenant with the Purchaser that they will not cause or permit any person directly or indirectly connected with them to do any of the things set out in clause 8.1.

8.3 The Vendors agree that, having regard to the facts and matters above, the restrictions contained in Clause 8.1 are reasonable and necessary for the protection of the legitimate interests of the Purchaser and that, having regard to those facts and matters, those restrictions do not work harshly on it. It is nevertheless agreed that, if any of those restrictions shall, taken together or separately, be held to be void or ineffective for any reason but would be held to be valid and effective if part of its wording were deleted, that restriction shall apply with such deletions as may be necessary to make it valid and effective.

8.4 The restrictions contained in the sub-clauses of Clause 8.1 shall be construed as separate and individual restrictions and shall each be capable of being severed without prejudice to the other restrictions or to the remaining provisions of this Agreement.

[9   Pensions

The provisions of Schedule 6 shall have effect.]

10   Confidentiality

10.1 No announcement of any kind shall be made about this Agreement by the Vendors or any parties controlled by them including their advisors and representatives and the transactions contemplated in it except as specifically agreed with the Purchaser or unless an announcement is required by the rules and regulations of a recognised investment exchange (as defined in the Financial Services Act 1986) or by law or by any taxation authority in which event the Vendors shall consult the Purchaser about the nature and content of such announcement.

10.2 With effect from the Completion Date The Purchasers shall be released from its obligations under a confidentiality agreement dated [ ] and accepted on [ ] between [ ] and [ ].

11   General

11.1 The Parties shall, and shall use their respective best endeavours to procure that any necessary third party shall, do and execute and perform all such further deeds, documents, assurances, acts and things as any of them may reasonably require by notice in writing to give effect to the terms of this Agreement.

11.2 This Agreement constitutes the entire agreement between the Parties with respect to the subject matter of this Agreement.

11.3 Each Party shall pay his or its own costs and expenses of and incidental to this Agreement and the sale and purchase of the Shares. The Vendors costs shall include any costs and expenses incurred by the Company and the Subsidiaries in connection with the transaction contemplated by this Agreement.

11.4 This Agreement shall, as to any of its provisions remaining to be performed or capable of having or taking effect following Completion, remain in full force and effect notwithstanding Completion.

11.5 This Agreement shall be binding upon and enure for the benefit of the successors and assigns of the Parties.

11.6 The Purchaser shall be entitled to assign the benefit (subject to the burden) of this Agreement to any transferee of the Shares (or part thereof) and, upon the request of the Purchaser, the Vendors agree to enter into a deed of novation on terms reasonably acceptable to the Purchaser for this purpose. The Vendors shall not be entitled to assign their respective rights or obligations under this Agreement without the previous written consent of the Purchaser.

11.7 The failure of the Purchaser at any time or times to require performance of any provision of this Agreement shall not affect its right to enforce such provision at a later time.

11.8 No waiver by the Purchaser of any condition nor the breach of any term, covenant, representation, warranty or undertaking contained in this Agreement, whether by conduct or otherwise, in any one or more instances shall be deemed to be or construed as a further or continuing waiver of any such condition or breach or a waiver of any other condition or deemed to be or construed as the breach of any other term, covenant, representation, warranty or undertaking in this Agreement.

11.9 This Agreement may be amended, modified, superseded or cancelled and any of its terms, covenants, representations, warranties, undertakings or conditions may be waived only by an instrument in writing signed by (or by some person duly authorised by) all of the Parties or, in the case of a waiver, by the Party waiving compliance.

11.10 No provision in this Agreement or in any of the Schedules to it (or in any document which may be executed pursuant to it or in connection with it) by virtue of which this Agreement is or may be registerable under the Restrictive Trade Practices Act 1976 (as amended) shall take effect until the day after particulars of this Agreement are furnished to the Director General of Fair Trading in accordance with the requirements of that Act.

11.11 Any liability to the Purchaser under this Agreement may in whole or in part be released, compounded or compromised or time or indulgence given by the Purchaser in its absolute discretion as regards any Party under such liability without in any way prejudicing or affecting its rights against any other Party under the same or a like liability, whether joint and several or otherwise.

11.12 At Completion the Vendors will assign to the Purchaser all rights that they may have pursuant to any confidentiality agreement entered into with third parties in connection with the possible sale of the Company.

11.13 All their obligations in this Agreement, the Tax Deed, the Environmental Deed and the Warranties are joint and several on the part of the Vendors.

12 Notices

12.1 Any notices required to be given under the provisions of this Agreement shall be in writing and shall be deemed to have been duly served if hand delivered or sent by facsimile or by first class registered or recorded delivery post within the United Kingdom and by registered airmail post outside the United Kingdom correctly addressed to the relevant party's address as specified in this Agreement or at such other address as either party may designate from time to time in accordance with this clause.

12.2 Any notice pursuant to clause 12.1 shall be deemed to have been served:-

12.2.1 if hand delivered at the time of delivery;

12.2.2 is sent by facsimile at the completion of transmission during business hours at its destination or if not within business hours at the opening of business hours at its destination on the next business day but subject to (1) proof by the sender that it holds a printed record confirming despatch of the transmitted notice and (2) despatch of the notice by post in accordance with clause 12.1 on the same day as its transmission; or

12.2.3 if sent by post within 48 hours of posting (exclusive of the hours of Sunday) if posted to an address within the country of posting and 7 days of posting if posted to an address outside the country of posting.

12.3 For the purpose of clauses 2.2 and 12.2 "business hours" means between 09.00 and 17.30 and "business day" means a day between Monday and Friday inclusive on which banks in the country of the addressee are open for business.

12.4 Service of a notice in accordance with clause 12.1 on [ ] shall be deemed to be service of that notice on [ ].

13 Governing Law and Jurisdiction

13.1 This Agreement shall be governed by and construed in accordance with the Laws of England.

13.2 The Parties submit to the non-exclusive jurisdiction of the English Courts as regards any claim, dispute or matter arising out of or relating to this Agreement or any of the documents to be executed pursuant to this Agreement.

SCHEDULE 1
THE COMPANY

1. Registered number: [ ]
2. Date of incorporation: [ ]
3. Place of incorporation: [ ]
4. Registered office address: [ ]
5. Directors: [ ]
6. Secretary: [ ]
7. Authorised share capital:
   a) Amount:
   b) Number and class of shares:
8. Issued share capital:
   a) Amount: £[ ]
   b) Number and class of shares: [ ]Ordinary Shares of £[ ]
9. Issued loan capital:
   a) Description:
   b) Amount:
10. Accounting Reference Date: [ ]
11. VAT Registration Number:
12. Auditors: [ ]
13. Bankers:
14. Shareholders: [ ]

SCHEDULE 2

THE SUBSIDIARIES

[Name of Subsidiary]

1. Registered number:
2. Date of incorporation:
3. Place of incorporation:
4. Registered office address:
5. Directors:
6. Secretary:
7. Authorised share capital:
   a) Amount:
   b) Number and class of shares:
8. Issued share capital:
   a) Amount:
   b) Number and class of shares and by whom held:
9. Issued loan capital:
   a) Description:
   b) Amount:
10. Charges:
    Date of charge:
    Date of Property registration:
    Sums secured:
    Chargee:
    Charged:
11. Accounting Reference Date:
12. VAT Registration Number:
13. Auditors:
14. Bankers:

Appendix 5

SCHEDULE 3
COMPLETION OBLIGATIONS OF THE VENDORS

At Completion, the Vendors shall deliver or procure to be delivered to the Purchaser:-

1. duly executed transfers in favour of the Purchaser or its nominee(s) in respect of the Shares together with the relative certificates;

2. any other document which may reasonably be required to give good title to the Shares or which may be necessary to enable the Purchaser to procure the registration of the same in the name of the Purchaser or its nominee(s);

3. a copy of any power of attorney under which this Agreement, or any of the transfers or other documents referred to in the preceding paragraphs 1 and 2 of this Schedule, is executed and evidence to the Purchaser's satisfaction of the authority of any person signing on behalf of any corporate entity;

4. the common seal and the share and other statutory books (including registers and minutes books) of the Company and the Subsidiaries made up to the Completion Date and all certificates of incorporation and certificates of incorporation on change of name of the Company and the Subsidiaries;

5. duly executed transfers in favour of the Purchaser or its nominee(s) in respect of any shares in the Subsidiaries which are not registered in the name of the Company or another of the Subsidiaries, together with the relative certificates;

6. letters of resignation in the Agreed Form marked "Cl" to "C [ ]" from [names of resigning directors and/or secretary] in each case acknowledging under seal that the writer has no claim against the Company or any of the Subsidiaries for compensation for loss of office or otherwise;

7. a copy of a letter from [ ] in the Agreed Form marked "C[ ]" resigning their office as Auditors of the Company and the Subsidiaries with effect from Completion and accompanied by the statement required by Section 394 Companies Act 1985, originals of such letter to be deposited at the registered office of the Company and the Subsidiaries and a written acknowledgement in the Agreed Form by such auditors that they have no outstanding claims against the Company and each Group Company;

8. engrossments in duplicate of the Tax Deed and the Environmental Deed duly executed [ ]

9. [engrossments in duplicate of each of the Service Agreements duly executed by the relevant Executive;]

10. [powers of attorney in the Agreed Form marked "Dl" to "D[ ]" duly executed by the Vendors;]

11. [deeds of release in the Agreed Form marked "El" to "E[ ]" duly executed by the Vendors;]

12. all credit cards in the name, or for the account, of the Company or any of the Subsidiaries in the possession of any officer or employee of the relevant company resigning at Completion;

13. the documents of title to the Properties [and any certificate(s) of title to be given in respect of any of the Properties];

14. evidence to the Purchaser's satisfaction of [the release and discharge of all charges and guarantees entered into by the Company and the Subsidiaries/the non-crystallisation of any floating charges created in favour of or by the Company and the Subsidiaries];

15. evidence to the Purchaser's satisfaction that debts and accounts between the Company and the Subsidiaries and any other member of [the Vendors' group] have been fully paid and settled and that there are no outstanding agreements or arrangements under which the Company or any of the Subsidiaries have or would have any obligation to any other member of the Vendors' group and vice versa;

16. appropriate certified minutes of each of the Vendors authorising execution of this Agreement, the Tax Deed, the Environmental Deed and any other ancillary documentation;

17. a certificate from the Company's and Group Companies' bankers certifying the current and deposit account balances of the Company and each Group Company at the close of business on the last business day preceding completion and a statement from the Company of all movements on all bank accounts since the date of such certificate(s);

18. the documentation relating to Intellectual Property Rights referred to in schedule 7;

19. all the current cheque books of each Group Company with forms to amend the mandates given to the relevant bank; and

20. executed agreements in the Agreed Form marked "H1" to "H4" between [ ] and the Purchaser:-

    (a) for the exclusive supply of equipment by [Company/Purchaser] to [ ];

    (b) relating to the Purchaser's first right of refusal to purchase business/shares of [ ].

SCHEDULE 4
THE WARRANTIES

1 DISCLOSED INFORMATION

1.1 Recitals and other Schedules

The facts set out in the Recitals and in Schedules 1 and 2 are true and accurate in all respects.

1.2 Memorandum and Articles of Association

The copy of the Memorandum and Articles of Association of the Company annexed to the Disclosure Letter is true and complete, has embodied in it or annexed to it a copy of every such resolution or agreement as is referred to in Section 380(4) Companies Act 1985 and sets out in full the rights and restrictions attaching to each class of the Company's share capital.

1.3 Statutory books

The statutory books (including all registers and minute books) of the Company have been properly kept and contain a complete and accurate record of the matters which should be dealt with in them and no notice or allegation that any of them is incorrect or should be rectified has been received.

1.4 Returns

All returns, particulars, resolutions and other documents required under the Companies Act 1985 and all other legislation to be delivered on behalf of the Company to the Registrar of Companies or to any other authority whatsoever have been duly and properly made and delivered.

1.5 Material disclosure

The Warranties (as modified by the Disclosure Letter) disclose all facts and circumstances relating to the Shares and to the assets, business and affairs of the Company material for disclosure to an intending purchaser of the Shares and, to the best of the knowledge, information and belief of the Vendors, there are no other facts or circumstances which render or which might upon their disclosure render any of such facts and circumstances misleading or which might reasonably affect the willingness of a purchaser to purchase the Shares on the terms (including price) of this Agreement.

2 THE VENDORS

2.1 Capacity

2.1.1 The Vendors have full power to enter into and perform this Agreement, the Tax Deed, the Environmental Deed and any other agreement which will need to be executed in connection with this transaction respectively and such documents will, when executed, constitute binding obligations of the Vendors in accordance with its terms and no third party or governmental consents or approvals are required.

2.1.2 The execution and delivery of the documents referred to in clause 2.1.1 by the Vendors and the performance of and compliance with their terms and provisions will not:-

2.1.2.1 conflict with or result in a breach of, or constitute a default under, any agreement or instrument to which it or the Company is a party or by which it or the Company is bound or of the Memorandum or Articles of Association of the Company;

2.1.2.2 conflict with or result in a breach of any law, regulation, order, writ, injunction, judgement or decree of any court or agency; or

2.1.2.3 cause the Company to lose the benefit of any right or privilege it presently enjoys or cause any person who normally does business with the Company not to continue to do so on the same basis or cause any officer or senior employee to leave and, so far as the Vendors are aware, the attitude or actions of customers, suppliers, employees and other persons with regard to the Company will not be prejudicially affected thereby.

2.2 Vendors' other interests

Neither the Vendors nor, any person connected with the Vendors has any interest, direct or indirect, in any business other than that now carried on by the Company which is or is likely to be or become competitive with the business or any proposed business of the Company.

3 THE SHARES AND THE COMPANY

3.1 The Shares

3.1.1 The Shares comprise the whole of the allotted and issued share capital of the Company and all of the Shares are fully paid up.

3.1.2 The Shares are beneficially owned by the Vendors free from all pre-emption rights, liens, charges, equities, encumbrances or interests of any nature whatsoever in favour of any other person.

3.2 Share and loan capital

Save only as provided in this Agreement, there are no agreements or arrangements in force which call for the present or future allotment, issue, sale or transfer of, or grant to any person the right (whether exercisable now or in the future and whether conditional or not) to call for the allotment, issue, sale or transfer of, any share or loan capital of the Company (including by way of option or under any right of conversion or pre-emption).

3.3 Company resolutions

Neither the Company nor any class of its members has during the period of six years ending on the date of this Agreement passed any Resolution (other than Resolutions relating to business at Annual General Meetings which was not special business).

3.4 Subsidiaries and subsidiary undertakings

3.4.1 The Company does not have, and never has had, any subsidiaries or subsidiary undertakings apart from the Subsidiaries or any interest in any partnership or unincorporated company or association.

3.4.2 The Company is the beneficial owner of the entire issued share capital of each of the Subsidiaries free from all pre-emption rights, liens, charges, equities, encumbrances or interests of any nature whatsoever in favour of any other person.

3.5 Associated companies

The Company has no associated companies as defined in SSAP I.

3.6 Foreign Branches

The Company has no branch, agency, place of business or permanent establishment or any substantial assets outside the United Kingdom.

4   THE ACCOUNTS AND ACCOUNTING RECORDS

4.1 The Accounts

The Accounts (a copy of which is annexed to the Disclosure Letter):-

4.1.1 comply with the requirements of the Companies Act 1985 as amended by the Companies Act 1989;

4.1.2 have been prepared in accordance with all applicable SSAPs and FRS's or, where there are none, in accordance with accounting principles generally accepted in the United Kingdom and on a basis consistent with preceding accounting periods;

4.1.3 show a true and fair view of the state of affairs of the Company as at the Accounts Date and of its profit or loss for the financial year ended on that date;

4.1.4 save as expressly disclosed in the Accounts, are not affected by any extraordinary, exceptional or non-recurring items;

4.1.5 fully disclose all the assets and liabilities (whether ascertained, contingent or otherwise and whether or not quantified or disputed) of the Company as at the Accounts Date and make full provision and/or reserve for all such liabilities; and

4.1.6 fully disclose all financial commitments in existence as at the Accounts Date.

4.2 Stock valuation

4.2.1 The method of valuing stock-in-trade and work-in-progress for the Accounts was in accordance with SSAP 9 and, subject to that Standard, was consistent in all respects with that adopted in the corresponding audited accounts for the preceding three financial periods and has been accepted by the Inland Revenue for taxation purposes.

4.2.2 Full provision has been made in the Accounts in respect of dead, slow moving, obsolete, redundant or excess stock-in-trade and/or work-in-progress and the value attributed to the remaining stock-in-trade and/or work-in-progress did not exceed the lower of direct cost or net realisable value at the Accounts Date.

4.3 Accounting records

The accounting records of the Company:-

4.3.1 have at all times been fully, properly and accurately kept and completed and contain due and accurate records of all matters required by law to be entered in them;

4.3.2 contain or reflect no material inaccuracies or discrepancies of any kind; and

4.3.3 give and reflect a true and fair view of the matters which ought to appear in them.

4.4 Management Accounts

The Management Accounts:-

4.4.1 give a true and fair view of the assets and liabilities of the [each Group] Company as at [ ] and its profits for the period from [ ] to [ ];

4.4.2 are not affected by any extraordinary exceptional or non-recurring item;

4.4.3 give a true and fair view of the financial position of the Company as at [ ];

4.4.4 fully disclose all the assets of the [each Group] Company as at [ ]; and

4.4.5 make proper provision or reserve for all liabilities and capital commitments of the [each Group] Company outstanding at [ ] including contingent unquantified or disputed liabilities.

5 TAXATION

5.1 Administrative matters

5.1.1 All computations, payments and returns which should have been made by the Company for any fiscal purpose have been made and are up-to-date, correct and made on a proper basis.

5.1.2 The Company has not at any time been, nor does it expect to be, involved in any dispute with, or the subject of any enquiry by, any branch of the Inland Revenue, H.M. Customs and Excise or other taxation authorities other than routine enquiries of a minor nature following the submission of computations and returns.

5.1.3　The Company has adequate records relating to past events to calculate any liability to Taxation or relief which would arise on any disposal, deemed disposal or realisation of any assets owned at the Accounts Date or acquired since that date but before the Completion Date.

5.1.4　The Company has duly and punctually paid all Taxation which it has become liable to pay and is under no liability to pay any penalty or interest in connection with any claim for Taxation. There are no amounts of Taxation in respect of periods up to the Accounts Date which remain unpaid at the date of this Agreement, whether the date for payment has passed or not.

5.1.5　The Company has submitted all claims, elections and disclaimers which have been assumed to have been made for the purposes of the Accounts.

5.2　Provision for Taxation in the Accounts
Full provision and reserves have been made in the Accounts in respect of all Taxation of any description liable to be assessed on the Company or for which it is accountable (including deferred taxation calculated according to the liability method) for accounting periods or fiscal years ended on or before the Accounts Date.

5.3　Base Values
If each of the capital assets of the Company were disposed of for a consideration equal to the book value of that asset in, or adopted for the purpose of, the Accounts, no liability to corporation tax on chargeable gains or balancing charge under CAA 1990 would arise (and for this purpose there shall be disregarded any relief and allowances available to the Company other than amounts falling to be deducted from the consideration receivable under Section 38 CGA 1992).

5.4　Replacement of business assets, etc.
The Company has not made, nor will it pending the Completion Date make, a claim under Sections 152 to 156 (inclusive) CGA 1992 and no such claim has been made by any other company under Section 175 CGA 1992 which affects, or could affect, the amount or value of the consideration for the acquisition of any asset by the Company and the provisions of Section 154 CGA 1992 do not apply to any such claim other than as is disclosed in the Disclosure Letter.

5.5　Close companies
The Company has not, at any time within the period of six years ending on the date of this Agreement, been a close company for the purpose of the ICTA.

5.6   Depreciatory transactions

5.6.1   No loss which might accrue on the disposal by the Company of any share in, or security of, any company or any other capital asset is liable to be reduced by virtue of any depreciatory transaction within the meaning of Sections 176 and 177 CGA 1992 and no gain is liable to be increased or deemed to have been made on such a disposal by virtue of such a transaction. No expenditure on any share or security is liable to be reduced under Section 125 CGA 1992.

5.6.2   The Company has not been involved in any transaction to which Sections 29 to 34 CGA 1992 may apply.

5.7   Chargeable gains

5.7.1   None of the Company's assets has been acquired for a consideration in excess of its market value at the date of such acquisition or otherwise than by way of a bargain at arm's length.

5.7.2   No liability to Taxation will arise on the disposal by the Company of any asset acquired since the Accounts Date for a consideration equal to that given on its acquisition. Nor has the Company been a party to any transaction since the Accounts Date which will give rise to a liability to corporation tax on chargeable gains.

5.8   Stamp Duty Reserve Tax, etc.

5.8.1   The Company has made all returns and paid all stamp duty reserve tax in respect of any transaction in securities to which it has been a party.

5.8.2   All documents to which the Company is a party and under which the Company has any rights or which form part of the Company's title to any asset owned by it or which the Company may need to enforce or produce in evidence in the courts of the United Kingdom have been duly stamped with the correct amount of Stamp Duty and (where appropriate) adjudicated.

5.9   Tax losses and ACT carry forward

5.9.1   There has been no change of ownership of the Company nor has there been any major change in the nature or conduct of a trade or business carried on by the Company, in each case within the meaning of Section 768 of the ICTA 1988 or Section 245 ICTA 1988.

5.9.2   Nothing has been done, and no event or series of events has occurred, which might cause the disallowance of the carry forward of losses or excess charges under the provisions of Section 393 ICTA 1988.

5.9.3   The amount of trading losses available to the Company for carrying forward has been, or will before the Completion Date be, agreed with the Inland Revenue and will not be less than £ [ ].

5.9.4 There are set out in the Disclosure Letter particulars of any surplus advance corporation tax being carried forward by the Company being advance corporation tax which has been surrendered to the Company concerned.

5.10 Value added tax

5.10.1 The Company:-

5.10.1.1 has complied in all material respects with all Taxation Statues relating to value added tax;

5.10.1.2 is not in arrears with any payment or returns, or liable to any abnormal or non-routine payment or to any forfeiture or penalty or to the operation of any penal provision in respect of value added tax;

5.10.1.3 has not applied for treatment as a member of a group of companies and no act or transaction has been effected in consequence of which the Company is or may be held liable for any value added tax chargeable against some other company;

5.10.1.4 is not and has not agreed to become an agent, manager or factor (for the purposes of Sections 47 and 48 VATA 1994) of any person who is not resident in the United Kingdom;

5.10.1.5 has not paid any value added tax to the Commissioners of Customs and Excise which is not tax due to them without making a claim for the recovery of that value added tax; and

5.10.1.6 has not been required by the Commissioners of Customs and Excise to give security.

5.10.2 The Disclosure Letter contains full particulars of any claim for bad debt relief made, or which may be made, by the Company under Section 36 VATA 1994.

5.10.3 The Company has not, within the period of one year preceding the date of this Agreement, received a surcharge liability notice under Section 59 VATA 1994 nor has the Company submitted a VAT return or payment later than the date prescribed for its submission.

5.10.4 The Company has not at any time received a penalty liability notice under Section 64 Finance Act 1994.

5.10.5 All supplies made by the Company are taxable supplies and the Company has not been and will not be denied credit for any input tax by reason of the operation of Section 26 VATA 1994 and regulations made under that Section.

5.10.6 The Company has not in the ten years preceding Completion incurred any expenditure on capital items such that the provisions of Part V of The Value Added Tax (General) Regulations 1985 may apply to the Company.

5.10.7 The Disclosure Letter contains full particulars of:-

5.10.7.1 any premises owned or occupied by the Company which may, at any date within the ten years following Completion, be subject to a `self supply' charge within paragraphs 5 and 6 of Schedule 10 VATA 1994 in the event that the Company makes an exempt supply;

5.10.7.2 any premises owned or occupied by the Company which are subject to an election under paragraph 2 Schedule 10 VATA 1994, whether made by the Company or by a relevant associate;

5.10.7.3 any agreement or other arrangement to which the Company is a party whereby the Company has agreed not to waive exemption from value added tax pursuant to Schedule 10 VATA 1994 in relation to any land;

5.10.7.4 any building or work (including any reconstruction or enlargement or extension of a building or work) within paragraph 5 Schedule 10 VATA 1994 in relation to which the Company is a "developer" whether currently under construction or where the construction was completed within a ten year period ended on Completion.

5.11 Import duties, etc.

All value added tax and excise duties payable upon the importation of goods in respect of any asset (including trading stock) imported or owned by the Company has been paid in full.

5.12 Distributions and payments

5.12.1 No distribution within the meaning of Section 210 ICTA has been made by the Company since 5th April, 1965. The Company is not bound to, and pending the Completion Date will not, make any such distribution.

5.12.2 No securities (within the meaning of Section 254(1) ICTA) issued by the Company and remaining in issue at the date of this Agreement were issued in circumstances such that the interest payable on those securities falls to be treated as a distribution under Section 209(2) ICTA. Nor is the Company under any obligation to make any payments of interest or any annual payments for which no tax relief will be received.

5.12.3 The Company has not made any deemed distributions within the meaning of Section 418 ICTA.

5.12.4 The Company has not at any time redeemed, repaid or purchased, or agreed to redeem, repay or purchase, any of its own shares.

5.13 Remuneration and benefits for employees

5.13.1 The Company has not made any payment to, or provided any benefit for or on behalf of, any officer or employee or ex-officer or ex-employee of the Company which is not allowable as a deduction in calculating the profits of the Company for taxation purposes.

5.13.2 The Company has not since [ ]paid any emoluments to any of its officers or employees more than nine months after the period to which those emoluments relate.

5.13.3 The Disclosure Letter contains full details of all share schemes (including those approved by the Inland Revenue and unapproved schemes) which the Company operates or in which UK employees are entitled to participate, together with copies of any approvals issued by the Inland Revenue in respect of such schemes and nothing has been done to prejudice the approved status of any such schemes.

5.13.4 The Disclosure Letter contains full details of any issue of shares or an interest in shares by the Company in the circumstances described in Section 138(1) ICTA or in Sections 77 to 89 Finance Act and the Company has complied with Section 139 ICTA 1988 and Section 85 Finance Act 1988 as appropriate.

5.13.5 The Company has properly operated the PAYE and National Insurance Contributions systems by making such deductions as are required by law, from all payments made or deemed to be or treated as made by it or on its behalf and by duly accounting to the Inland Revenue for all sums so deducted and for all other amounts for which it is required to account under the PAYE and National Insurance Systems.

5.14 Transfer of overseas trade
The Company has not transferred a trade, carried on by it outside the United Kingdom through a branch or agency, to a company not resident in the United Kingdom in circumstances such that a chargeable gain may be deemed to arise at a date after such transfer under Section 140 CGA 1992.

5.15 Secondary Liability

5.15.1 No transaction or event has occurred in consequence of which the Company is or may be held liable for any taxation or deprived of any relief or allowance otherwise available to it or may be otherwise held liable for any taxation for which some other company or person was primarily liable (whether by reason of any such other company being or having been a member of the same group of companies or otherwise).

5.15.2 There is no liability (including a contingent liability) of the Company which arises under Section 190 CGA 1992 in respect of any chargeable gain which has accrued or may accrue to the Company.

5.16 Group Relief and ACT

5.16.1 The Disclosure Letter contains true and complete particulars of all arrangements and agreements relating to group (including consortium) relief (as defined by Sections 402 and 413 ICTA 1988) to which the Company is or has been a party and:-

5.16.1.1 all claims by the Company for group relief were when made and are now valid and have been or will be allowed by way of relief from corporation tax;

5.16.1.2 the Company has not made nor is liable to make any payment under any such arrangement or agreement save in consideration for the surrender of group relief allowable to the Company as in paragraph 5.16.1.1; and

5.16.1.3 the Company has received all payments due to it under any such arrangement or agreement for surrender of group relief made by it and no such payment is liable to be refunded in whole or in part.

5.16.2 The Disclosure Letter contains true and complete particulars of all arrangements and agreements to which the Company is or has been a party relating to the surrender of advance corporation tax made or received by the Company under Section 240 ICTA 1988 and the Company:-

5.16.2.1 has not paid nor is liable to pay for the benefit of any advance corporation tax which is or may become incapable of set-off against the Company's liability to corporation tax; and

5.16.2.2 has received all payments due to it under any such arrangement or agreement for all surrenders of advance corporation tax made by it and no such payment is liable to be refunded in whole or in part.

5.16.3 The Accounts do not reflect any claim for group relief or for advance corporation tax surrendered to the Company for which a formal surrender or consent has not been submitted to and agreed by the Inland Revenue.

5.16.4 The provisions of Section 409(2) ICTA 1988 do not apply to the Company so as to permit the apportionment of profits and losses to be made otherwise than on a time basis according to the respective lengths of the component accounting periods.

5.17 Intra-group transfers

5.17.1 The Company has not at any time acquired any assets from another company which was at any relevant time a member of the same group of companies (as defined in Section 170 CGA 1992) as that of which the Company was also a member or an associated company as defined in Section 774 ICTA 1988.

5.17.2 The Company has not carried out or been engaged in any transaction or arrangement to which the provisions of sections 770 ICTA have been or may be applied.

5.18 Group income election

A group income election under Section 247 ICTA 1988 has been made and remains in force.

5.19 Anti-avoidance

The Company has not at any time been a party to or otherwise involved in:-

5.19.1 a transaction or series of transactions containing steps in respect of which it or its advisers considered or ought to have considered that there was a risk that the Company could be liable to taxation under the provisions of Part XVII ICTA 1988 or as a result of the principles enunciated by the House of Lords in Furniss v Dawson 55 TC 324; or

5.19.2 any scheme or arrangement of which the main purpose or one of the main purposes was the avoidance of, or a reduction in liability to, Taxation.

6 ASSETS

6.1 Title to assets and encumbrances

6.1.1 Except for trading stock sold by the Company in the ordinary course of its day to day business or for trading stock acquired subject to retention or reservation of title by the supplier or manufacturer of such trading stock as disclosed in the Disclosure Letter, all the assets included in the Accounts or acquired after the Accounts Date as well as all the assets used in the Company's business and all the IP Rights (as defined in paragraph 6.5.1 of this Schedule):-

6.1.1.1 are owned by the Company with good and marketable title free from any mortgage, charge, lien or other encumbrance;

6.1.1.2 are not held subject to any agreement for lease, hire, hire purchase or sale on conditional or deferred terms; and

6.1.1.3 are in the possession or under the control of the Company.

6.1.2 In respect of any of the items referred to in the preceding paragraph 6.1.1 which are held under any agreement for lease, hire, hire purchase or sale on conditional or deferred terms, there has been no default by the Company in the performance or observance of any of the provisions of such agreements.

6.2 Plant

6.2.1 The plant and machinery, including fixed plant and machinery, and all vehicles and office and other equipment used in connection with the business of the Company:-

6.2.1.1 are in good repair and condition and in satisfactory working order;

6.2.1.2 have been regularly and properly maintained;

6.2.1.3 are not surplus to the Company' s requirements;

6.2.1.4 are in its possession and control and are its absolute property except for those items the subject of the hire purchase leasing or rental agreements referred to in the Disclosure Letter;

6.2.1.5 are not expected to require replacements or additions at a cost in excess of £10,000 within six months after Completion; and

6.2.1.6 are all capable and (subject to normal wear and tear) will remain capable through the respective periods of time during which they are each written down to nil value in the accounts of the Company (in accordance with the normal recognised accountancy principles consistently applied prior to the date hereof) of doing the work for which they were designed or purchased.

6.2.2 Maintenance contracts are in full force and effect in respect of all assets of the Company which it is normal or prudent to have maintained by independent or specialist contractors and in respect of all assets which the Company is obliged to maintain or repair under any leasing or similar agreement.

6.2.3 All the assets referred to in paragraph 6.2.2 have been regularly maintained to a good technical standard and in accordance with safety regulations usually observed in relation thereto and in accordance with the terms and conditions of any applicable leasing or similar agreement.

6.2.4 No plant, machinery, furniture, fixtures, fittings, furnishings or other equipment located at any of the Properties or used by the Company in its business is owned by the Vendors or any person connected with the Vendors.

6.2.5 Details of all new equipment contracts in the process of installation are provided in the Disclosure Letter.

6.3 Stock

6.3.1 The stocks of raw materials, packaging materials and finished goods now held are not, to the best of the Vendors' knowledge and belief, excessive and are adequate in relation to the current trading requirements of the business of the Company.

6.3.2 The Company's stock in trade is in good condition and is capable of being sold by the Company in the ordinary course of its business in accordance with its current price list without rebate or allowance to a purchaser.

6.4 Debts

6.4.1 The amount of all debts recorded in the Accounts or the books of the Company as being due to the Company (less the amount of any specific provision or reserve for such debts made in the Accounts) will be received in full in the ordinary course of business and in any event not later than three months after the Completion Date and none of those debts is subject to any counter-claim or set-off.

6.4.2 No part of the amounts included in the Accounts or (in the case of an amount arising after the Accounts Date) in the books of the Company as due from debtors has been released on terms that any debtor pays less than the full book value of his debt or has been written off or has proved to any extent irrecoverable or is now regarded as irrecoverable.

6.4.3 If any of the debts recorded in the Accounts or the books of the Company or any of the Subsidiaries as being due to the Company or any of the Subsidiaries at Completion ("the Debts") shall not have been recovered in full within the period of three months following the Completion Date, the Vendors shall immediately when called upon in writing to do so by the Purchaser (and shall (if not so called upon) be entitled to) purchase the Debts from the Company or the relevant Subsidiary for an immediate cash consideration equal to the full face value of the Debts and the Purchaser shall, on payment of such consideration, procure the assignment of the Debts to the Vendors (or as they may direct) absolutely and such payment shall operate as a discharge of the liability of the Vendors arising by reason of the non-payment of the Debts within the period mentioned above.

6.4.4 A complete list of the Debts is attached to the Disclosure Letter.

6.5   Intellectual property

6.5.1   For the purposes of this sub-paragraph, the following expressions shall have the following meanings:-

"IP Rights" rights in patents, petty patents, trademarks, service marks, registered designs, design rights, trade names, copyright, topography rights and all other intellectual property in respect of which exclusive rights can exist, and including applications for any such rights;

"Third Party IP Rights" IP Rights owned otherwise than by the Company including IP Rights owned by the Vendors;

"Confidential Information" information held subject to express agreement or implied obligations as to confidentiality and information of value to the Company and not generally known outside the Company.

6.5.1.1   Particulars of all IP Rights owned or used by the Company are set out in Part 1 of Schedule 7 and particulars of all Third Party IP Rights used by the Company are set out in Part 2 of Schedule 7 including any licence granted by the Company, and any assignment, and any information disclosed by the Company in the last ten years in relation to such IP Rights.

6.5.1.2   The basis on which the Company uses Third Party IP Rights has been disclosed to the Purchaser in the Disclosure Letter, including all liability for payment which may be outstanding or may accrue after the Completion Date, and any restrictions on use.

6.5.1.3   Those products, processes and information used or owned by the Company in respect of which it has Confidential Information have been disclosed to the Purchaser with details of all the Confidential Information and the form in which it is held. All such products, processes and information shall remain the property of the Company and the Vendors shall not keep any copy or derivative materials thereof.

6.5.1.4   The basis on which the Company uses Confidential Information not owned by it is disclosed in the Disclosure Letter, including details of all liability for payment which may be outstanding or may accrue after the Completion Date and any restrictions on use.

6.5.1.5   The business and activities of the Company have not required, nor do they now require, the agreement or licence of any third party in order to avoid infringement by the Company of any Third Party IP Rights or Confidential Information.

6.5.1.6 The Company has not been in breach of, and is not now in breach of, and Completion will not result in any breach of any agreements concerning Third Party IP Rights or Confidential Information.

6.5.2 No claims (including, without limitation, any civil or criminal actions, administrative proceedings and any other proceedings) have been made or threatened against the Company or its customers:-

6.5.2.1 by any third party concerning IP Rights or Confidential Information;

6.5.2.2 by any supplier to or employee of the Company concerning moral rights or employee rights to compensation regarding patents; or

6.5.2.3 by way of opposition to any application by the Company for registration of IP Rights, or seeking cancellation of any of the Company's IP Rights, or for a licence of right, or otherwise adversely affecting any of the Company's IP Rights.

6.5.3 No licences or registered user agreements have been entered into by the Company in respect of IP Rights owned by it, nor is the Company obliged to enter into any such or to grant assignments of any IP Rights held by it.

6.5.4 The Company has not disclosed Confidential Information to any party except under obligations of confidentiality.

6.5.5 The Company owns or is licensed to use and is in possession of all IP Rights and Confidential Information necessary or customarily used in its business without the payment of any sums to any party subject to the particulars in Schedule 7 and as necessary to manufacture all supply products pursuant to the agreements referred to in item 20 of Schedule 3.

6.5.6 The Vendors do not and have not provided services to the Company in the last five years which cannot be performed by the Company in the same manner without the payment of fees exceeding what was previously paid.

6.5.7 All computer outsourcing or shared services agreements are listed in Schedule 7 together with their particulars.

6.6 Properties

6.6.1 The Properties comprise all the freehold, leasehold or other real property owned, occupied or otherwise used by the Company. There are attached to the Disclosure Letter details of all unoccupied properties for which the Company is responsible and all properties formerly occupied by the Company in respect of which the Company may have any liability, contingent or otherwise.

6.6.2 The Company is in physical possession and actual and exclusive occupation of the whole of each of the Properties and has quiet enjoyment thereof and there is no lease sublease tenancy service occupancy or licence affecting the Properties other than those particulars of which are correctly summarised in [ ] nor is there any person in occupation or possession of or who has or claims any right or easement of any kind in respect of the Properties.

6.6.3 The particulars of each of the Properties set out in Schedule 5 are true and accurate in all respects.

6.6.4 The Company has good and marketable title to each of the Properties and is the sole legal and beneficial owner of each of them.

6.6.5 The Company has in its physical possession all of the title deeds and documents which properly constitute title to each of the Properties and which are originals or properly examined abstracts. No title deeds or documents to any of the Properties are missing or incomplete.

6.6.6 The Properties are free from and not affected by any mortgage or charge (whether legal or equitable, specific or floating), debenture, lien, pledge or other security interest or other encumbrance whatsoever, including without limitation any which secure the payment of monies or other obligation or liability of any third party.

6.6.7 All covenants, stipulations, obligations, restrictions or similar encumbrances affecting the Properties have been strictly observed and performed and no notice or complaint has been received or served by or upon the Company is respect of any breach or alleged breach of any such matter and there is no outstanding dilapidations liability contingent or otherwise.

6.6.8 There is no matter, event or thing which would be revealed by the searches and enquiries which would be carried out by a prudent purchaser of the Properties and/or which are known to the Company which adversely affect the use and enjoyment of the Properties for the use set out in Schedule 5 or the title held to the Properties.

6.6.9 The Properties enjoy all necessary rights and are not affected by any disputes of any kind.

6.6.10 The Properties are in a good state of repair and condition and contain no dangerous or deleterious substances and will not require material expenditure in the foreseeable future.

6.6.11 In relation to each of the Properties which are leasehold:-

6.6.11.1 [the leases under which the Properties are held are correctly summarised in [Schedule 5] and the current rent therein quoted is duly evidenced by memoranda];

6.6.11.2 the Company has paid the rent and observed and performed the covenants and agreements on the part of the tenant (none of which are onerous or unusual) and the conditions contained in any leases, and in any licences or other documents supplemental to or granted under any leases, and has obtained all consents required for the grant of such leases;

6.6.11.3 all rents have been reviewed at the times and in the manner specified in the leases and there are no rent reviews in the course of being determined or otherwise outstanding or unimplemented at the date hereof;

6.6.11.4 there are no rights for the lessors of the Properties to determine any of the leases of the Properties other than by way of forfeiture for non payment of rent or breach of covenant [or insolvency of the tenant];

6.6.11.5 all persons entitled to any reversionary interest in the Properties or any right over or affecting the Properties have complied with any obligations and restrictions upon them and no such obligations have been waived

6.6.12 The Company does not have any actual or contingent liability in respect of any freehold or leasehold property which was previously but is not presently owned, whether under restrictive or other covenants as original tenant or as guarantor, assignee or otherwise, nor any liability or contingent liability for dilapidations.

6.6.13 The Properties have appropriate means of access from a public highway and this is held as a matter of right.

6.6.14 The Company has complied with all statutory and other requirements whatsoever whether relating to pollution or protection of the environment (including emissions, releases, or discharges of any kind whatsoever) or otherwise and the Company has no knowledge of any notice being received from any local or public authority which may affect the rights of the Company in relation to the Properties and no circumstances exist by virtue of which the service of such notices is warranted or likely.

6.6.15 The present user of the Properties is the permanent and unconditional permitted user thereof under the Town and

Country Planning Act 1994 and no development within the meaning of such Act has taken place or been commenced upon the Properties and the said Act and all other legislations and regulations relating to Town and Country Planning and fire regulation requirements have in all respects been complied with and the use and occupation of the Properties is in all respects lawful and there is no outstanding monetary claim or liability contrary or otherwise under such Act or legislation.

6.6.16 All statutory municipal and other requirements applicable to any licences and contracts (including planning consents) involved in the use and enjoyment of the Properties now used and enjoyed have been complied with and there is no intended or contemplated refusal or revocation of any such licence or consent.

6.7 Environmental matters and pollution

6.7.1 The Company has at all times carried on its business in all respects in compliance with all Environmental Laws.

6.7.2 The Company:-

6.7.2.1 has all necessary licences, authorisations, approvals and consents required by Environmental Law to enable it lawfully to carry on its business as presently carried on by it and all licences, authorisations, approvals and consents are currently in full force and effect;

6.7.2.2 has complied with all such licences, authorisations, approvals and consents including, without limitation, any conditions, limitations and directions imposed on such licenses, authorisations, approvals and consents and any subsequent amendment, alteration and order relating to them;

6.7.2.3 has taken all necessary or appropriate action in connection with the renewal, continuation or extension of all such licences, authorisations, approvals and consents including, without limitation, the payment of all sums necessary such as annual fees and application fees; and

6.7.2.4 is not required by any governmental organisation to incur any expenses, make any investment or carry out any improvements or other works by the terms of any such licences, authorisations, approvals and consents or in order to renew or maintain the same in full force and effect.

6.7.3 No event has occurred or circumstance exists which entitles, and nothing is proposed to be done or is likely to occur, which would entitle any licence, authorisation, approval and consent referred to in paragraph 6.7.2.1 whether in part or in whole to be revoked, suspended, amended, varied, withdrawn or not renewed or which would prevent compliance with any terms of any such licence, authorisation, approval or consent.

6.7.4 No application for or the surrender or variation of the terms of any licence, authorisation, approval or consent referred to in paragraph 6.7.2.1. or the transfer of such licence, authorisation, approval or consent to or from the Company, is pending or has been refused for any reason.

6.7.5 There has been no breach and there is no existing breach by the Company or any director, secretary, manager or other similar officer of the Company or any other person who was purporting to act in such capacity, or any of the Company's members of any Environmental Laws.

6.7.6 No civil, criminal or administrative claim, accusation, allegation, notice of violation, demand, cause of action, abatement or other order (conditional or otherwise), has been made or brought against or served on the Company, or any director, secretary, manager or other similar officer of the Company or any other person who was purporting to act in such capacity, or any of the Company's members or any former owner or occupier of any of the Properties in respect of any Environmental Law or any other person in respect of any Environmental Law relating to the Company and there are no facts or matters which could or might form the basis of any such claim, accusation, allegation, notice of violation, demand, cause of action or abatement or other order.

6.7.7 No regulatory body, court, organisation or other person has given any notice to the Company prohibiting, suspending, or requiring the halting of all or any part of any activity keeping or process carried out by the Company, whether or not on any of the Properties or requiring any remedial action, repair, improvement, modification or other works to be carried out, in order that any activity keeping or process may continue and the Vendors are not aware of any act, omission or circumstance which could or might give rise to an entitlement or obligation to give such a notice.

6.7.8 The Company has not deposited, disposed of, kept, treated, imported, exported, transported, processed, manufactured, collected, sorted or produced or caused or consented to the presence of any Hazardous Material (whether or not on any of the Properties) and to the best of the knowledge information and belief of the Company no other person has at any time deposited, disposed of, kept, treated, imported, exported, transported, processed, manufactured, collected, sorted or produced or caused or consented to the presence of any Hazardous Material on any of the Properties.

6.7.9 Neither the Company nor any other person (whether or not on behalf of the Company) has conducted any environmental inspection, investigations, studies, audits, tests, reviews or other analyses in relation to the Company or the business carried on at the Properties.

6.7.10 The Company has not carried on and does not intend to carry on a process or emit any substance which is prescribed by the Secretary of State pursuant to section 2 Environmental Protection Act 1990 and in respect of which the Company did not or does not have a valid current authorisation under that Act.

6.7.11 The Company has not carried on any manufacturing or other process, mineral extraction or deposit keeping, storage, or treatment of Waste on any of the Properties which has resulted in the contamination or pollution of the soil, surface water or ground water on or adjacent to such Property or of any public sewer.

6.7.12 There is nothing in, on or under and there has been nothing in, on or under the Properties which may cause or may have caused contamination or pollution of the Environment or harm to human health.

6.7.13 There are no deposits or accumulations of Hazardous Materials in, on or under the Properties.

6.7.14 The Properties are not referred to or listed and are not likely to be referred to or listed in any register of land which may be polluted or contaminated, kept or to be kept pursuant to any Environmental Laws.

6.7.15 No process is or has been carried out on the Properties which may result or may have resulted in trade effluent or commercial or industrial waste requiring or which required disposal or the emission of any substance into the air or the discharge of any substance into any water.

6.7.16 The Company has adequate environmental insurance cover.

6.7.17 The Company has complied at all times with the Health and Safety at Work etc. Act 1974 and all regulations relating to Health and Safety and has not received any notice or complaint from any employee of the Company in respect of Regulations and no circumstance exists which is likely to place the Company in breach of Regulations.

Appendix 5

7 EMPLOYEES AND CONSULTANTS

7.1 Directors

The particulars of Directors shown in paragraph 5 of Schedule 1 and in paragraph 5 of each Part of Schedule 2 are true and complete and no person not named as such in that paragraph is or is held out as a director of the Company.

7.2 Particulars of employees

7.2.1 The particulars shown in the Schedule of Employees annexed to the Disclosure Letter show all remuneration payable and other benefits provided or which the Company or the Vendors are bound to provide (whether now or in the future) to each officer and employee of the Company and/or any person connected with any such person and include true and complete particulars of all profit sharing, incentive and bonus arrangements to which the Company is a party, whether legally binding on the Company or not, and no person not named in that Schedule is an employee of the Company.

7.2.2 Since the Accounts Date, no change has been made in the rate of remuneration or the emoluments or pension benefits of any officer, ex-officer or employee of the Company and no change has been made in the terms of engagement of any such officer or employee and no additional officer or employee has been appointed.

7.2.3 No present officer or employee of the Company has given or received notice terminating his employment, except as expressly contemplated under this Agreement.

7.2.4 The Company has not entered into any agreement or arrangement (express or implied) for the provision of compensation on the termination of employment of any employee of the Company beyond the minimum required by law.

7.2.5 The Disclosure Letter contains full details of all redundancy payments made by the Company in the three years preceding the date of this Agreement. No such payments exceed the statutory minimum.

7.3 Service contracts

7.3.1 There is not now outstanding any service contract between the Company and any of its directors, officers or employees which is not terminable by the Company without compensation (other than statutory compensation) on one month's notice or less given at any time.

7.3.2 The attention of all employees of the Company has been drawn to such of the terms of their employment as is required by the Employment Rights Act 1996 (as amended).

7.4 Trades unions

The Company is not a party to any agreement or arrangement with or commitment to any trades union or staff association nor, to the best of the Vendors' knowledge, information and belief, are any of its employees members of any trades union or staff association.

7.5 Disputes with employees

7.5.1 There is no outstanding claim against the Company by any person who is now or has been an officer or employee of the Company or any dispute between the Company and a material number or class of its employees and no payments are due by the Company under the provisions of the Employment Rights Act 1996 (as amended) or the Wages Act 1986.

7.5.2 No employee or officer of the Company has been involved in any accident, or any incident for which the Company may be vicariously liable, during the last 12 months.

7.6 Consultants

There is not now outstanding any contract or arrangement to which the Company is a party for the payment to any person or body of any consultancy or like fees.

7.7 Ex-gratia payments

Since the Accounts Date, no ex-gratia payments have been made by the Company to any officer or employee or former officer or employee of the Company or to their dependants or relatives nor is the Company considering making any such payments.

7.8 Pensions

7.8.1 The Company has no obligation (whether legally binding or not) to:-

7.8.1.1 pay any pension; or

7.8.1.2 make any other payment after retirement or death or during periods of sickness or disability (whether of a temporary or permanent nature); or

7.8.1.3 otherwise to provide "relevant benefits" (within the meaning of Section 612 ICTA 1988) to, or in respect of any person who is now or has been an officer, director or employee of the Company or spouse or dependant or other person claiming through said officer, director or employee or employees membership of the Scheme or employment with the Company.

7.8.2 Save in respect of the [ ] ("Scheme"), the Company is not a party to or obliged to contribute to any scheme or arrangements having as its purpose or one of its purposes the making of any such payments or the provision of any such benefits, and there are no closed or paid up schemes providing such benefits.

7.8.3 No change in the benefits currently being provided under the Scheme has been announced by the Company or is being considered by it nor is any change (statutory or otherwise) intimated as being imposed upon the Company and Trustees of the Scheme.

7.8.4 No undertaking or assurance has been given to any person who is now or has been an officer, director or employee of the Company or spouse or dependant of such officer, director or employee as the continuance or introduction or improvement of any benefits referred to in this Warranty.

7.8.5 Full details of the Scheme have been disclosed to the Purchaser and accurate, up-to-date and complete copies of the following documents are annexed to or contained in the Disclosure Letter:-

7.8.5.1 all documents constituting or relating to the Scheme;

7.8.5.2 a full list of active members, deferred pensioners and pensioners;

7.8.5.3 a full list of all part time members of the Scheme and confirmation part time members have part time members have pensionable service since 1976

7.8.5.4 the names and addresses of the trustees and of the actuary of the Scheme; and

7.8.5.5 the latest actuarial valuation and report.

7.8.6 There are fully disclosed in the Disclosure Letter details of:-

7.8.6.1 the rates of discretionary increases granted to pensions in payment or in deferment under the Scheme in the 10 years prior to the date of this Agreement;

7.8.6.2 details of any discretionary practises operated on a regular basis in relation to the Scheme under which individuals are provided with additional or increased benefits in specified circumstances; and

7.8.6.3 details of the rates of credited interest applicable for each year prior to the date of this Agreement.

7.8.7 All information which has been made available to the Purchaser or its advisers on or before the date of this Agreement is true, complete, accurate and fairly presented.

7.8.8 The Scheme is an "exempt approved scheme" (within the meaning of Chapter I of Part XIV ICTA) and has at all times complied with and been administered in accordance with all applicable laws, regulations and requirements, including the requirements of the Inland Revenue for continued approval as an exempt approved scheme and of trust law. There is no reason why approval of the Scheme by the Board of Inland Revenue should be withdrawn.

7.8.9 The provisions of the Scheme do not directly or indirectly discriminate between male and female members as regards eligibility, the rate of contributions, the amount of any benefits provided or the date on or from which such benefits will or may be provided.

7.8.10 All benefits (other than a refund of members' contributions with interest where appropriate) payable under the Scheme on death before normal pension age in respect of any person whilst in an employment to which the Scheme relates are fully insured under a policy with an insurance company of good repute. All contracts of insurance relating to the Scheme are enforceable and there is no ground on which the insurers might avoid liability.

7.8.11 No employer other than the Company (and specified essential confirms) has ever participated in the Scheme.

7.8.12 The liability of the Company to contribute to the Scheme can be terminated by the Company without notice, without the consent of any person and without further payment.

7.8.13 There is contained in or annexed to the Disclosure Letter a statement of the amounts and rate of contributions to the Scheme during the period of five years ending on the date of this Agreement. There has been no alteration and no reduction to the rate of contributions to the Scheme or the method of calculating the amount to which that rate of contributions is applied during that five year period.

7.8.14 Contributions to the Scheme are not paid in arrears and all contributions to and expenses of the Scheme which have fallen due for payment have been paid. A list of all expenses of the Scheme is annexed to or contained in the Disclosure Letter together with an indication in each case as to the person or persons liable to pay such expenses. No services have been rendered in respect of the Scheme in respect of which an account or other invoice has not been rendered.

7.8.15 No power to provide enhanced or new benefits under the Scheme has ever been exercised in relation to any employee or officer currently in the service of the Company nor has any such power been exercised in relation to any other employee or officer since the day before the date as at which the last actuarial valuation of the Scheme was undertaken nor is there any arrangement (whether legally binding or not) to provide enhanced or new benefits in a given set of circumstances (by way of example, but without limitation, on employees retiring from service at the request of the Company or in the event of them, or those of them who are over a specified age, being made redundant) and the Company is not considering implementing any such arrangement.

7.8.16 The Scheme is a defined benefit scheme.

7.8.17 The total amount or value of the funds subject to the trusts of the Scheme is equal to or exceeds, and does not fall short of, the total liabilities (actual or contingent) in respect of benefits payable or to be payable to members or past members of the Scheme, such liabilities being calculated on the basis of actuarial and financial assumptions used in the latest actuarial valuation of the Scheme including (with respect to liabilities for benefits calculated by reference to remuneration at or averaged over a period ending on a member's normal retirement date or date of death) the assumption as to the levels of such remuneration at such date. The Scheme currently has free assets available to meet the requirements of actuarial guidelines GN11 and full cash equivalent transfer payments can be effected in respect of all members.

7.8.18 No repayment of assets or monies of the Scheme has been or is proposed to be made by the trustees of the Scheme to any employer participating in the Scheme.

7.8.19 There is no dispute with regard to the benefits payable under the Scheme and no legal proceedings, including any complaint to or investigation by the Pensions Ombudsman or the Occupational Pensions Advisory Service Limited by or against the trustees of the Scheme in their capacity as such are pending, threatened or expected and there is no fact or circumstance likely to give rise to any such proceedings.

7.8.20 Claims for incentive payment under Section 7 Social Security Act 1986 have been made in respect of any qualifying members of the Scheme and such incentive payments shall be included in the transfer values available to members transferring to the Purchaser's Scheme (if applicable)

7.8.21 The Company has at all times complied with all the provisions of the Scheme which apply to it. Full records, accounts and minutes of meetings of the trustees of the Scheme have been properly and accurately maintained at all times and the Scheme has at all times been administered in accordance with its governing documentation and relevant UK and European law.

7.8.22 The Scheme holds no securities issued by, properties leased to or occupied by, and has made no loans which are at the date of this Agreement outstanding to the Company or any other employer who participates in the Scheme and there are no charges over any of the assets of the Scheme.

7.8.23 The Company does not participate in any retirement benefit scheme or similar arrangement established under or regulated by the laws of any jurisdiction outside the United Kingdom.

7.8.24 The Scheme has taken appropriate steps to comply with the provisions of the Pensions Act 1995 and can comply fully with the new provision of the Act due to come into effect on 6th April 1997.

8 LIABILITIES AND COMMITMENTS

8.1 Material contracts

8.1.1 The Company is not a party to or subject to any agreement, transaction, obligation, commitment, understanding, arrangement or liability which:-

8.1.1.1 is incapable of complete performance in accordance with its terms within six months after the date on which it was entered into or undertaken;

8.1.1.2 is likely to result in a loss to the Company on completion of performance;

8.1.1.3 cannot readily be fulfilled or performed by the Company on time without unusual expenditure of money and effort;

8.1.1.4 involves or is likely to involve obligations, restrictions, expenditure or receipts of an unusual, onerous or exceptional nature;

8.1.1.5 is a forward contract relating to foreign currency;

8.1.1.6 involves or is likely to involve the supply of goods by or to the Company the aggregate sales value of which exceeds £[ ];

8.1.1.7 is a contract for services (other than a contract for the supply of electricity, gas or water or normal office services);

8.1.1.8 requires the Company to pay any commission, finders' fee, royalty or the like;

8.1.1.9 in any way restricts the Company's freedom to carry on the whole or any part of its business in any part of the world in such manner as it thinks fit;

8.1.1.10 is an agreement or arrangement otherwise than by way of bargain at arm's length;

8.1.1.11 is in any way otherwise than in the ordinary and proper course of the Company's business;

8.1.1.12 is an agreement that creates a joint venture or partnership with any other person or entity;

8.1.1.13 is an indenture, mortgage, note, bond or other evidence of indebtedness, any credit or similar agreement under which it has borrowed any money, or any guarantee of or agreement to acquire any such obligation of any other person or entity, involving a principal amount in excess of £[ ];

8.1.1.14 is an agreement for the construction or modification of any building or structure or for the incurrence of any other capital expenditure involving amounts in excess of £[ ]; or

8.1.1.15 is an agreement relating to the acquisition or disposal of a material amount of assets (by way of merger, consolidation, purchase, sale or otherwise) pursuant to which the Company may have any future obligations (including, without limitation, any indemnification obligations).

8.1.2 All agreements referred to in the Disclosure Letter in relation to paragraph 8.1.1 are valid and enforceable and complete copies of such agreements are attached to the Disclosure Letter.

8.2 Defaults

Neither the Company nor any other party to any agreement with the Company is in default under any such agreement nor (so far as the Vendors are aware) are there any circumstances likely to give rise to such a default.

8.3 Sureties

No person apart from the Company has given any guarantee of or security for any overdraft, loan or loan facility granted to the Company or in connection with any trading activities of the Company.

8.4 Powers of attorney/agency

8.4.1 There is in force no power of attorney or other authority (express, implied or ostensible) given by the Company to any person to enter into any contract or commitment on its behalf other than to its employees to enter into routine trading contracts in the usual course of their duties.

8.4.2 The Company has not appointed any agent or distributor in respect of any of its products or services in any part of the world.

8.5 Insider contracts

8.5.1 There is not outstanding, and there has not at any time during the six years ending on the date of this Agreement been outstanding, any agreement or arrangement to which the Company is a party and in which any Vendors, any person beneficially interested in the Company's share capital, any director of the Company or any person connected with any of them is or has been interested, whether directly or indirectly.

8.5.2 The Company is not a party to, nor have its profits or financial position during such period been affected by, any agreement or arrangement which is not entirely of an arm's length nature.

8.6   Debts

There are no debts owing by the Company, other than debts which have arisen in the ordinary course of business.

8.7   Borrowings and mortgages

8.7.1   The Company has no borrowings, and has not agreed to create any borrowings, from its bankers or any other source and, in respect of borrowings disclosed in the Disclosure Letter, the Company has not exceeded any limitation on its borrowing contained in its Articles of Association or in any debenture or loan stock deed or other instrument.

8.7.2   No option, right to acquire, mortgage, charge, pledge, lien (other than a lien arising by operation of law in the ordinary course of business) or other form of security or encumbrance or equity on, over or affecting the whole or any part of the undertaking or assets of the Company is outstanding and there is no agreement or commitment to give or create any.

8.8   Third party indebtedness

The Company is not subject to any option or pre-emption right or a party to any guarantee or suretyship or any other obligation (whatever called) to pay, purchase or provide funds (whether by the advance of money, the purchase of or subscription for shares or other securities, the purchase of assets or services, or otherwise) for the payment of, indemnity against the consequences of default in the payment of, or otherwise to be responsible for, any indebtedness of any other person.

8.9   Tenders etc.

No offer, tender or the like is outstanding which is capable of being converted into an obligation of the Company by an acceptance or other act of some other person.

8.10   Trade warranties

8.10.1   The Company has not given any guarantee or warranty or made any representation in respect of articles or trading stock sold or contracted to be sold by it, save for any guarantee or warranty implied by law and (save as aforesaid) has not accepted any liability or obligation to service, repair, maintain, take back or otherwise do or not do anything in respect of any articles or stock which would apply after any such articles or stock have been delivered by it.

8.10.2   The Company has not manufactured, sold or supplied any products or services which are or were or will become in any material respect faulty or defective or which do not comply with any warranties or representations expressly or impliedly made by the Company or with any applicable regulations, standards and requirements.

8.10.3 All visits at service sites in respect of maintenance and repairs have been made strictly in accordance with contractual requirements and have been properly logged.

8.11 Litigation

8.11.1 Neither the Company, nor any person for whose acts or defaults the Company may be vicariously liable, is involved in any civil, criminal or arbitration proceedings or governmental investigation and no such proceedings or investigation are pending or threatened by or against the Company or any such person and, so far as the Vendors are aware, there are no facts or circumstances which are likely to lead to any such proceedings.

8.11.2 No judgment has been obtained against the Company which has not been satisfied.

8.11.3 Details of all claims made by or against the Company exceeding £[ ]together with all settlements in relation to any claims in the last six years are set out in the disclosure letter.

9 THE COMPANY'S BUSINESS

9.1 Business since the Accounts Date
Since the Accounts Date:-

9.1.1 the Company has carried on its business in the ordinary and usual course and without entering into any transaction, assuming any liability or making any payment not provided for in the Accounts which is not in the ordinary course of its business and without any interruption or alteration in the nature, scope or manner of its business;

9.1.2 the Company has not borrowed or raised any money or taken any financial facility;

9.1.3 the Company has paid its creditors within the times agreed with such creditors;

9.1.4 the Company has not entered into, or agreed to enter into, any capital commitment nor has it disposed of or realised any capital assets;

9.1.5 no share or loan capital has been allotted or issued or agreed to be allotted or issued by the Company;

9.1.6 no distribution of capital or income has been declared, made or paid in respect of any share capital of the Company and (excluding fluctuations in overdrawn current accounts with bankers) no loan or loan capital or preference capital of the Company has been repaid in whole or part or has become liable to be repaid;

9.1.7   there has been no depletion in the net assets of the Company; and

9.1.8   there has been no change or event materially and adversely affecting the business, results of, operation or financial position including the cash and accounts receivable account, turnover or prospects of the Company.

9.1.9   the Company has not taken any action which, if taken after the date of this Agreement, would require the Purchaser's consent pursuant to clauses 6.1. to 6.4.

9.2   Working Capital
The Company has sufficient working capital for the purpose of continuing to carry on its business in its present form and at its present level of turnover and for the purposes of executing, carrying out and fulfilling in accordance with their terms all existing orders, projects and contractual obligations which have been placed with, or undertaken by, the Company.

9.3   Grants
The Company has not applied for or received any grant or allowance from any authority, agency or governmental organisation.

9.4   Compliance with laws
The Company is entitled to carry on the business now carried on by it without conflict with any valid right of any person, firm or company and the Company has conducted its business in all material respects in accordance with all applicable laws and regulations of the United Kingdom or any foreign country and there is no violation of, or default with respect to, any statute, regulation, order, decree or judgment of any Court or any governmental agency of the United Kingdom or any foreign country.

9.5   Licences
All necessary licences, consents, permits and authorisations (public or private) have been obtained by the Company to enable the Company to carry on its business effectively in the places and in the manner in which such business is now carried on and all such licences, consents, permits and authorisations are valid and subsisting and the Vendors, after due and careful enquiry, know of no reason why any of them should be suspended, cancelled or revoked.

9.6   Insolvency
9.6.1   No order has been made and no resolution has been passed for the winding up of the Company or for a provisional liquidator to be appointed in respect of the Company and no petition has been presented and no meeting has been convened for the purpose of winding up the Company.

9.6.2   No administration order has been made and no petition for such an order has been presented in respect of the Company.

9.6.3 No receiver (which expression shall include an administrative receiver) has been appointed in respect of the Company or all or any of its assets.

9.6.4 The Company is not insolvent or unable to pay its debts within the meaning of Section 123 Insolvency Act 1986 nor has it stopped paying its debts as they fall due.

9.6.5 No voluntary arrangement has been proposed under Section 1 Insolvency Act 1986 in respect of the Company.

9.6.6 The Company has not been a party to any transaction at an undervalue as defined in Section 238 Insolvency Act 1986 nor has it given or received any preference as defined in Section 239 Insolvency Act 1986, in either case within the period of two years ending on the date of this Agreement.

9.6.7 No event analogous to the foregoing has occurred in or outside England.

9.6.8 No unsatisfied judgement is outstanding against the Company.

9.6.9 No guarantee, loan capital, borrowed money or interest is overdue for payment and no other obligation or indebtedness is outstanding which is substantially overdue for performance or payment.

9.7 Fair trading

9.7.1 No agreement, practice or arrangement carried on by the Company or to which the Company is a party or with which the Company is concerned:-

9.7.1.1 is or requires to be registered in accordance with the provisions of the Restrictive Trade Practices Acts 1976 and 1977 or contravenes the provisions of the Resale Prices Act 1976 or is or has been the subject or any enquiry, investigation or proceeding in respect thereof;

9.7.1.2 is proscribed by or has been the subject of an enquiry, investigation, reference or report under the Fair Trading Act 1973 (or any previous legislation relating to monopolies or mergers) or the Competition Act 1980;

9.7.1.3 infringes Article 85 of the Treaty of Rome or constitutes an abuse of dominant position contrary to Article 86 of that Treaty or infringes any regulation or other enactment made under Article 87 of that Treaty or is or has been the subject of any enquiry, investigation or proceeding in respect thereof;

9.7.1.4 is, by virtue of its terms or by virtue of any practice for the time being carried on in connection with it, a "consumer trade practice" within the meaning of Section

13 Fair Trading Act 1973 and susceptible to or under reference to the Consumer Protection Advisory Committee or the subject of a report to the Secretary of State for Trade and Industry or of an Order by the Secretary of State for Trade and Industry under the provisions of Part II of that Act; or

9.7.1.5 infringes any other competition, restrictive trade practice, anti-trust or consumer protection law or legislation applicable in the United Kingdom or elsewhere and not specifically mentioned in this paragraph 9.7.

9.7.2 The Company has not given any undertaking or assurance to the Restrictive Practices Court or the Director General of Fair Trading or the Secretary of State for Trade and Industry or the Commission or Court of Justice of the European Community or to any other court, person or body and is not subject to any Act, decision, regulation, order or other instrument made by any of them relating to any matter referred to in this paragraph 9.7.

9.7.3

9.8 Insurances

9.8.1 The Company and all its normally insurable assets are, and at all times have been, covered to their full replacement or reinvestment value by valid insurances containing no special or unusual terms or conditions against all the risks (including in the case of let property for three years' loss of rent) against which it is normal or prudent to insure and all liabilities of the Company in respect of the business carried on by it (including third party risks, public and employers' liability, consequential loss liability and loss of profits) are fully covered and the Company has paid all premiums due and has not done or omitted to do anything the doing or omission of which would make any such policy of insurance void or voidable or would or might result in an increase in the rate of premiums payable under any such policy.

9.8.2 Where any of the Properties which are leasehold are insured by the landlord under the relevant lease, the interest of the Company is noted on the insurance policy.

9.8.3 The Schedule of Insurances annexed to the Disclosure Letter contains full details of:-

9.8.3.1 the insurance policies of the Company or in which it has an interest;

9.8.3.2 all excesses and deductibles pertaining to such policies;

9.8.3.3 all claims made under such policies and provisions by the insurer made against those policies in the five years preceding the date of this Agreement;

9.8.3.4 all premiums paid in respect of such policies in the five years preceding the date of this Agreement;

9.8.3.5 all policies of insurance taken out by the Company in the last 20 years covering employers liabilities and public and product liability; and

9.8.3.6 any onerous or exceptional insurance requirements in any leases to which the Company is a party.

9.9 Customers and suppliers

9.9.1 During the period of five years ending on the date of this Agreement:-

9.9.1.1 the Company has not lost any major or substantial customer for or supplier of all or any of its products or services or requirements;

9.9.1.2 no major or substantial customer has significantly reduced its orders for all or any of the products or services of the Company;

9.9.1.3 there has been no substantial change (apart from normal price changes) in the basis or terms on which any person is prepared to enter into contracts or do business with the Company;

and no such loss, reduction or change is anticipated whether as a result of Completion or otherwise.

9.9.2 Neither in the financial period ending on the Accounts Date nor in the period since then has any person (together with other persons connected with him) purchased from, or sold to, the Company products or services exceeding £[ ]in value and there is no person (together with other persons connected with it) on whom the Company is substantially dependent or the cessation of business with whom would substantially affect the business of the Company.

9.9.3 There are no service or maintenance contracts on which the Company makes or is projected to make a margin of less than [ ] per cent. and the average margin of all such service and maintenance contracts is not less than [ ] per cent. For the purposes of this warranty margin means the revenue from such service or maintenance contract less the direct costs incurred by the Company (being the cost of the Company's labour, supervisor and materials used specifically for such servicing or maintenance).

9.9.4 The revenue generated from the Company's maintenance contracts for the accounting period ended on the Accounts Date was not less than £[ ].

9.9.5 The revenue generated by the Company's contracts for repairs and modernisation services for the accounting period ended on the Accounts Date was not less than £[ ].

9.9.6 There is attached to the Disclosure Letter complete and accurate details of all the contracts referred to in paragraphs 9.9.4 and 9.9.5 of this schedule, such details to include a contract number, date of signature, duration, price and type of contract. Such contracts are valid and enforceable and the Company is not in default of any of them.

9.10 The Company's activities, etc.

None of the activities, contracts or rights of the Company is ultra vires, unauthorised, invalid or unenforceable or in breach of any contract or covenant and all documents in the enforcement of which the Company may be interested are valid and have been duly stamped.

10 CONSEQUENCES OF SALE OF THE SHARES

10.1 Other agreements and obligations

Neither the Vendors nor the Company is a party to any agreement or bound by any obligation the terms of which will prevent the Purchaser from enjoying the full benefit of this Agreement.

10.2 Change of control

There are no agreements concerning the Company which will or may be terminated or the terms of which will or may in any way be varied or would otherwise require consent as a result of a change in the control of the Company or in the composition of the Board of Directors of the Company.

10.3 Finders fee

No brokers or finders fee or commission payment will be payable by the Vendors or the Company as a result of this Agreement.

SCHEDULE 5
THE PROPERTIES

1. Registered Land

Freehold:

Brief Description	Registered Proprietor	Title Number	Present Use

Leasehold:

Brief Description	Registered Proprietor	Title Number	Original Partners	Date of Lease & Unexpired Term	Current Rent	Present Use	Rates Payable	Service Charges Paid for Last Year

2. Unregistered Land

Freehold:

Brief Description	Estate Owner	Date of Conveyance to Estate Owner	Parties	Present Use

Leasehold:

Brief Description	Estate Owner	Date of Conveyance to Estate Owner	Parties	Present Use

3. Other Property Worldwide

Brief Description	Country in which Situated	Owner	Present Use

[SCHEDULE 6
PENSIONS]

SCHEDULE 7
INTELLECTUAL PROPERTY

Part I

All cases

Identify where application has been made but not granted and details of proposed applications.

Patents, petty patents

Title; Proprietor; Country of grant; Number; Priority date; Date of grant; Renewal date; Licensees; Licence of right entered.

Trade Marks, service marks

Mark (copy in the case of logo/device); Proprietor; Country of grant; Number; Date of registration; Class number; Goods/Services for which registered; Details of disclaimers or restrictions; Licensees; Registered users; Next renewal date; Associated marks;

Registered designs

Design title; Proprietor; Country of grant; Number; Application date; Date of grant; Licensees; Next renewal date;

Trade Names/Copyright/Topography rights/Design right

Rights concerned (name; work in copyright; topography description); Proprietor; Countries where protection exists; Date created; Authorship; Whether author created work in course of employment; Licensees; Waivers of moral rights.

Confidential Information:

List disclosure of Confidential Information provided by and to the Company and documentation covering confidentiality.

Part II
Third Party IP Rights

Computer Software Licences

Details of licenses and users, including Vendors licences used by the Company.

Outsourcing Agreements and Arrangements

(Including shared usage of computer and administration services.)

Others

For each item:

Documents evidencing ownership and/or usage of the above to be handed over at Completion/attached to the Disclosure Letter.

SCHEDULE 8

(AGREED FORMS)

1   Management Accounts
2   Tax Deed
3   Environmental Deed
4   Board Minutes (Completion)
5   Disclosure Letter
6   [Service Agreements]
7   [Letters of Resignation (Directors/Secretary)]
8   [Letter of Resignation (Auditor)]
9   [Powers of attorney]
10 Agreements with [ ] and pre-emption rights (see paragraph 20 of schedule 3)

SCHEDULE 9

AGREED ACCOUNTING PRINCIPLES

Appendix VI

Capital Gains Tax
Reinvestment Relief

Trading activities not eligible for relief

a) Any activity that is not commercially undertaken with a view to profit

b) Dealing in land, in commodities or futures, or in shares, securities or other financial instruments

c) Property backed ventures such as Nursing Homes, Farming and property development

d) Dealing in goods other than in the course of an ordinary trade of wholesale or retail distribution

e) Banking, insurance, money-lending, debt-factoring, hire purchase financing or other financial activities

f) Leasing (including ship chartering) or receiving royalties or licence fees

g) Providing legal or accounting services

h) Providing services or facilities for a trade carried on by someone else (other than its holding company) whose activities consist, to a substantial extent, of activities within (b) to (g) and a controlling interest in whose trade is held by a person who has a controlling interest in the trade of the company providing the services or facilities.

Appendix VII

Capital Gains Tax on Sale of a Business

Retirement Relief Summary

- Available for individuals who have attained the age of 50 at the time of disposal: relief at a younger age is given in the case of serious ill health.

- Individuals need to have worked in the business for ten years to obtain the full relief. For periods less than ten years the relief is reduced pro rata.

- Disposal of the whole or part of a trading business or shares in a trading company if there is a minimum ownership of 25% (or 5% if working full-time in the business).

- Individual does not need to retire to obtain relief.

- Abolished on disposals after 5th April 2003.

Rates:

	Amount of Gain	
Tax Year	First Slice: 100% exempt £	Second Slice: 50% exempt £
1998/99	250,000	750,000
1999/00	200,000	600,000
2000/01	150,000	450,000
2001/02	100,000	300,000
2002/03	50,000	150,000

Taper Relief Summary

- Applicable on disposals after 5th April 1998 depending on number of years asset has been held.

- Where asset was held on 17th March 1998 a bonus year is added to the number of years held.

- Additional relief is available for business assets such as those used in a trade or shares in a trading company if there is a minimum ownership of 25% (or 5% if working full-time in the business).

- The appropriate taper relief rate is used to reduce the capital gain which is subject to tax.

Rates:

Number of complete years asset held	Business Taper Relief	Non-Business Taper Relief
0	0%	0%
1	7.5%	0%
2	15%	0%
3	22.5%	5%
4	30%	10%
5	37.5%	15%
6	45%	20%
7	52.5%	25%
8	60%	30%
9	67.5%	35%
10 or more	75%	40%

The following table shows the amount of tax payable by an individual on £1,000,000 of capital gains assuming that the asset was held on 17th March 1998, and is a 40% taxpayer with no other capital gains or losses.

Tax Year	With retirement relief Tax payable £	Without retirement relief Tax payable £	Tax rate on gains over £1m
1998/1999	136,030	367,280	37%
1999/2000	167,280	337,280	34%
2000/2001	191,030	307,280	31%
2001/2002	207,280	277,280	28%
2002/2003	216,030	247,280	25%
2003/2004	217,280	217,280	22%
2004/2005	187,280	187,280	19%
2005/2006	157,280	157,280	16%
2006/2007	127,280	127,280	13%
2007/2008	97,280	97,280	10%
2008/2009	97,280	97,280	10%

Appendix VIII

Glossary

Alternative Investment Market (AIM)
Stock Exchange for smaller companies. Has less regulation than the London Stock Exchange.

Asset-stripping
Buying a company, and then selling its surplus assets to produce an overall profit on the transaction. Sometimes the parts of a business are worth more than the whole.

Banker's draft
A guaranteed cheque issued by and in the name of a bank which cannot be cancelled. As good as cash.

BIMBO
Buy-In Management Buy Out: A combined MBI and MBO.

Completion
When the Sale and Purchase Agreement becomes effective and the purchaser owns the company.

Completion meeting
Where the seller and purchaser meet with their respective solicitors to effect the Sale and Purchase Agreement – not a simple affair, this can often take a whole day or more.

Confidentiality undertaking
An agreement by prospective purchasers to keep confidential any information they may receive on your business and not to use it except in evaluating your business. It also usually includes an undertaking to return any information when requested to do so and confirm that no copies have been made. It sometimes contains an indemnity for damages resulting from unauthorised use. However, in practice these rights can be difficult to enforce.

Consideration
The total amount you are receiving for the sale of the business. It may include a non-cash element, such as shares in the acquiring company.

Deferred consideration
Where part of the total price of your business is paid at a future date.

Disclosure Letter
A document prepared by you and your solicitor detailing specific facts about the business so that in the future the purchaser cannot claim no knowledge of them.

Dividend strip
Payment of a dividend before selling, either to reduce the price paid by the purchaser or to maximise the net of tax receipts of the vendor.

Due diligence
The investigation into your company's affairs by the purchaser or his financiers. Usually undertaken by accountants and solicitors.

Earn-out
Where part of the price you receive for your business is dependent upon the size of future profits.

Earnings per share (EPS)
The after tax profit of a company divided by the number of shares in issue.

Engrossment
Final, fully agreed, bound Sale and Purchase Agreement ready for signature.

Equity
The share capital of a company or the value belonging to the shareholders.

Gearing
Level of borrowings of a business in relation to equity.

Goodwill
The price paid for a business above the value of its net assets.

Heads of Agreement
An outline of the main points agreed between the vendor and the purchaser. May or may not be binding.

Hive-down
Transferring selected assets or activities of a company to a new subsidiary. Usually, the subsidiary is then sold.

Indemnities and Warranties
A legally binding guarantee that specific information you have given the purchaser about your business is not false or incomplete.

Information Memorandum
A document designed to give a prospective purchaser enough information on your business to decide whether to proceed. A selling document.

Leveraged buyout
Buying a business using a lot of borrowed money.

Loan notes
A formal loan agreement, usually with pre-set repayment dates, with a specified rate of interest.

Lock-out
An agreement with a prospective buyer not to proceed with negotiation/sale to anyone else for a specified period.

Mezzanine finance
High risk lending, usually fairly short term where the lender does not have a first charge or debenture. In return, he expects a high rate of interest and usually, some kind of equity interest.

MBI
Management buy-in. Where an individual or a team of people buy a business to run it themselves, usually with a lot of borrowed money.

MBO
Management buy-out. Where the business is sold to the existing management, usually with a lot of borrowed money.

Net assets
The value of all the assets of a business less all its liabilities. Also known as Shareholders' funds.

Ofex
A type of Stock Exchange run by a firm of stockbrokers buying and selling shares on a matched deal basis.

P/E ratio
Price/earnings ratio: a shorthand way of assessing the value of the business in terms of the number of years it takes to recover the purchase price out of its after-tax profits.

Prospectus
See Information Memorandum. Can mean a formal document prepared in accordance with 1985 Companies Act.

Reinvestment Relief
The reinvesting of a capital gain into shares in an eligible trading business so as to defer payment of capital gains tax.

Reporting accountants
The accountants employed by the prospective purchaser to undertake due diligence (q.v.) and to report thereon.

Restrictive covenants
Typically, your agreement not to compete for an agreed period with the business you have sold.

Retirement relief
The savings of capital gains tax on selling a business after the age of 50 or earlier if for health reasons.

Rollover relief
Deferring part or all of the capital gains tax on the sale of a business by accepting shares or loan stock in the acquiring company instead of cash.

Sale and Purchase Agreement
The legally binding document detailing the agreement between the seller and the purchaser: it sets out who is selling what to whom for how much and when.

Section 151
The general prohibition in the 1985 Companies Act of a company giving financial assistance for the purchase of its own shares except in specific circumstances.

Senior debt
Bank or similar loans where the lender has a first charge or debenture.

Shareholders' funds
See Net assets.

Vendor finance
Where the seller agrees to loan back to the company some of the sale proceeds or accept deferred consideration.

Vendor placing
Where the purchaser, which is a quoted company, issues its own shares for an acquisition which are immediately sold on the Stock Exchange to produce the agreed cash price for the seller.

Venture capital
Investment capital, typically offered with low security but requiring a high anticipated rate of return.

Appendix IX

MacIntyre Corporate Finance

MacIntyre Corporate Finance provides a full range of corporate finance services including advice on disposals, acquisitions, fund raising and MBOs/MBIs. We are also able to act as quasi-financial directors for owner-managed businesses.

Disposals

MacIntyre Corporate Finance specialises in the disposal of UK and international companies. We work closely with clients to maximise the value of the business prior to sale. Having produced an appropriate information memorandum on the business, we use our industry contacts to identify and develop a list of buyers that are suitable to achieve your objectives.

Our role then moves on to the negotiation stage when we give advice on all aspects of the transaction. Structuring the actual deal is a crucial part of our disposal work and it is particularly important to ensure that clients receive the right tax advice.

We give you a total "hand-holding" service from the initial stages right through to the final signing and we are always there to provide professional (and emotional!) support throughout the sale. We recognise that this is probably the most important financial transaction of your life and it has got to be right.

Acquisitions

Focused planning is essential in any corporate acquisitions strategy and our extensive experience helps clients to develop all necessary plans and ensure that the acquisition is exactly what they expected.

After the planning stage we are able to compile a list of potential opportunities and once the suitable business is identified MacIntyre Corporate finance helps with the negotiations and provides a commercial full due diligence service. Our tax advice is also geared to structuring the deal in the most efficient way.

Fund raising

When our clients ask us to help them raise funds for a business venture, we invariably begin the process by carefully appraising the overall project. After this stage, we can work together to draw up business plans and projections that achieve the right end result.

Our knowledge of the sources of finance that are available to business, in addition the traditional bank financing, means that our clients have access to the full range of potential funds. This wide choice of funding options combined with our expertise in the area of tax structures enables clients to raise finance in the most efficient and effective way possible.

MBOs/MBIs

Whichever side you are on in a management buy-out or buy-in, you will need to be aware of the issues. This method of "transferring" the ownership of a business is unlike the traditional acquisition/disposal route, with different hurdles that need to be overcome.

We have practical commercial experience of advising our clients on structuring MBOs and MBIs and we use this knowledge to help them avoid the potential pitfalls. Right through the transaction we are closely involved in the deal, helping to find the right structure for everyone to work with, achieving both commercial and tax efficiency.

International capability

As a member of an international network of independent professional advisers, MacIntyre Sträter International Limited (MSI), MacIntyre Corporate Finance provides corporate finance services to clients around the world. We advise overseas buyers on UK based transactions and we are in a strong position to assist UK businesses with their international deals.

Quasi-Financial Director ("QFD")

There are a wide variety of reasons why many owner-managed businesses find the need for a quasi-financial director. Our QFD services provide the combination of independent professional advice and an in-house "sounding board" with actual hands-on experience of the business and how it works. As a result, the business benefits from strategic financial advice and taxation consultancy that can help to predict any issues that may affect the business before they happen. We may not have a crystal ball but we do have a deep understanding and personal experience of owner-managed businesses and their financial operations.

How to contact us

If you would like to find out how your business could benefit from any of our corporate finance services, please contact Gary Morley, Guy Rigby, or Eric Dunmore at MCF on T: 0171 430 0000 or F: 0171 404 9709.

Index

Order book, 54

P/E ratio, 29, 55
Planning, 19
Potential, 56
Preparing for Sale, 19-22
Price, 45-61
Price-Earnings ratios ("P/E"),
  29, 55
Private expenditure, 20
Profits, 21
  growth, 26
  history, 57
Property leases, 54
Purchaser, 57
  finding, 23-35

Quality of earnings, 59

Researching potential
  purchasers, 33

Restrictive covenants, 80
Risk, 46

S.151 of the Companies Act
  1985, 48
Sale and Purchase Agreement,
  75-81, 117-176
Share price, 25
Size, 60
Solicitors, 15, 67, 76, 80
Spouse, 19
Staff, 21, 24-26, 29, 37, 53, 65

Taxation, 69-73, 177--181

Vendor Politics, 63-67
Venture Capitalists, 30

Warranties, 78, 128